THE POWER
OF RUDE

THE POWER OF RUDE

A woman's guide to asserting herself

REBECCA REID

First published in Great Britain in 2020 by Trapeze
an imprint of The Orion Publishing Group Ltd
Carmelite House, 50 Victoria Embankment
London EC4Y 0DZ

An Hachette UK Company

1 3 5 7 9 10 8 6 4 2

A CIP catalogue record for this book is
available from the British Library.

ISBN (Trade Paperback) 978 1 4091 9530 6
ISBN (eBook) 978 1 4091 9532 0

Printed and bound in Great Britain by Clays, Ltd, Elcograf, S.p.A.

MIX
Paper from
responsible sources
FSC® C104740

www.orionbooks.co.uk

CONTENTS

This book is dedicated to me,
because I wrote it.

And Lucy,
because she really needs to read it.

A NOTE ON LANGUAGE

The Power of Rude is based on my experiences and those of the women I interviewed for the book, who were predominantly straight or bisexual; therefore when the book addresses romantic relationships it tends to assume that the couple consists of a man and a woman. This is not to suggest that heterosexual relationships are the 'right' or 'normal' type, just that they are the most common, and therefore what most women experience.

Similarly, in writing the book, in order to avoid the repetition of 'women and non-binary people' and 'women in heterosexual relationships' (which is clunky and would have thrown the word count), I worked on the basis that 97 per cent and 98 per cent of the population are cis and bisexual or straight, respectively; but while this is a large majority, it is important to point out that it is not an entirety.

Much of the experience of learning to be rude is tied up with being socialised as a woman from birth, and, in the chapters about dating and sex, being a straight woman. We know that gay women report higher relationship satisfaction and have more fulfilling sex lives, therefore the advice in the dating and sex chapters is mostly for straight women, who are much more in need of it. If you're not having sex with men, skip the sex and dating chapters and allow yourself a moment of smugness.

Using standardised language throughout the book was intended for simplicity and ease of reading, not exclusion or erasure.

METHODOLOGY

In order to gather as much information about women's attitude to being rude as possible, I put together a comprehensive anonymous survey which invited women from anywhere in the world to answer specific yes or no questions, as well as to contribute answers of unlimited length; 152 women took part.

The survey was shared widely outside my own networks, but I wanted to make sure that I wasn't just representing people from my age group or location. I interviewed fifteen women who were aged over forty, as the majority of the respondents to the survey were under forty.

I also spent a lot of time sitting in cafés or travelling on buses, listening to women talk to each other. As a naturally nosy person I found it perfectly normal, but other people have expressed horror at this method. It was, however, enormously useful in terms of observing the dynamics between women, as well as testing my hypothesis that women from all backgrounds and of all ages were struggling not to seem rude on a daily basis.

A NOTE ABOUT THE STORIES IN THIS BOOK

There were times when writing *The Power of Rude* that I worried I was coming across as pathetic or spineless. And when I asked women to share their stories, most of the responses were the same: women emailed me to say, 'I didn't realise how often I did this until I wrote it all down. I'm disappointed in myself.'

The aim of collating their stories wasn't to portray women as helpless, spineless or weak – though, reading them uncharitably and in sequence, you could perhaps reach that conclusion. It's important to remember that every woman will have a handful of these accounts and that in this book they are magnified because they have all been placed next to each other.

It's also important to acknowledge that sometimes, as is evident in these stories, women have made the wrong choice. They've placed the fear of seeming rude above whatever it was they actually wanted.

We have a collective phobia as women – especially as younger women – of being perceived as rude. Sometimes that means we pay for a mediocre meal or a lopsided haircut. At other times it means we're passed over for promotion or suffer through sex that we don't want. And if we're going to change that, then we're going to have to start being honest about it.

It is not unfeminist to acknowledge that women are fallible, and that sometimes we get things wrong. We are products of a society which pressurises us to behave in a certain way, and changing the status quo takes a lot of thought, effort and time. Some days you just don't have it in you to be a warrior, and that's OK.

I am enormously grateful to all of the women, both strangers and friends, who shared their stories of times when they've got things wrong, taking the path of least resistance and losing out through a fear of being rude. Their names have, for the most part, been changed, because these generally aren't things that they feel proud of, and who they are is not relevant.

It is not my aim to portray women as weak or place them in an unfavourable light, but rather to reflect the reality of life when a fear of being rude has been drilled into you from childhood. I hope it will help us all to think about our language and behaviour in a different way.

HAVE YOU EVER?

Your problem areas won't be exactly the same as mine. But have you ever:

- Paid in full for a terrible meal.
- Lain awake while your neighbours played their music full-blast.
- Taken the stairs at double speed because someone is behind you.
- Pretended to forget that a friend owes you money.
- Kept a gift you hated instead of asking for the receipt.
- Pretended to be in a relationship to avoid a flirty stranger.
- Laughed along with a joke which really hurt your feelings.
- Put away someone else's equipment at the end of a gym class.
- Stayed silent when someone jumped a queue you're waiting in.
- Kept your seat upright on a flight while the person in front of you is fully reclined.
- Let your friend bring a boyfriend to a girls' night.
- Routinely cleaned up after your housemate.

If you've done, or regularly do, any of the above, then you've come to exactly the right place.

They might seem insignificant, and in isolation they are. But if you do a handful of these little things each week out of a desire to avoid being rude, by the end of any given week, the list of ways in which you have twisted yourself around other people's wants and needs is a mile long. 'The power of rude' is the name I've given to the ability to step outside that pattern of behaviour.

The last 100 years have seen incredible progress for women, and, in terms of the rights we have enshrined in law, things look better than they ever have. Never has feminism been more popular, widespread or well represented. Emma Watson, Beyoncé, Taylor Swift – the vast majority of famous women identify as feminists. People like me make a living out of being feminist. And yet I, and women all over the world, still continue to experience sexism day in, day out.

The pay gap endures, maternity rights and childcare provisions can still lock women out of the workplace. We still experience sexual violence in obscene numbers, girls are still street-harassed before they leave childhood. Reproductive freedom is under attack and contraceptive medicine still makes women mentally and physically ill. Many of the world's most powerful nations have still never had a female leader. So, despite being stamped on tote bags and pink pencils, necklaces and T-shirts, feminism's work isn't finished. The war for women is not won.

I suspected before I wrote this book that, as a woman, perhaps the best way to improve my world would be by making small changes to my own behaviour. By the time I finished it, I was sure. If we want to continue the feminist revolution that was started by the Suffragettes, then we need to tackle the expectations to which we conform without really meaning to – most importantly of all, the expectation that we women will smile sweetly, sit nicely, take up as little space as possible and put our own wants and needs last, for fear of seeming rude.

When I started writing *The Power of Rude*, I decided to keep a diary noting down every time I did something because I didn't want to be rude. I thought I would need to keep it for several weeks in order to notice any patterns, but from the very first day my problems were clear.

Tuesday

8.30 a.m.
I wake up and realise that I didn't set my alarm. I'm running late so I call an Uber to take me to work, which cuts the journey time in half.

9.00 a.m.
I get into the taxi. It's way too hot, but he seems to like it this way, so I start stripping off layers. I consider opening the window but decide against it. He tunes the radio to a noisy sports game. I have a headache but assume this is an important match that he would be sad to miss, so again I say nothing. When I arrive at work, I feel embarrassed about having taken an Uber and hope no one sees.

9.30 a.m.
If I get a coffee from the coffee shop, I will be four minutes late into the office, but much more productive. I don't have the balls to style it out, so skip the coffee. I am sleepy through my next two meetings as a result.

10.15 a.m.

One of the writers I edit files a piece which hasn't really hit the mark, but I like her too much to say anything, so rewrite it myself.

1 p.m.

Lunch! Earlier in the week I batch-cooked a curry and a soup. My husband asked which one I wanted, I claimed I didn't mind, even though I did, and have ended up with the soup. I curse myself as I plough through it.

2.30 p.m.

One of the team members whom I technically manage (though I have a strong tendency towards the Regina George's mum school of people management) takes ninety minutes for lunch. When she comes back, I say, 'Everything OK?', which is designed to be code for 'Why are you so late?'. 'Everything's fine!' she smiles.

5.30 p.m.

I have finished all of the things that I need to do for the day and come to a natural conclusion. I could easily go home, but I'm worried someone will notice and think that I'm lazy, so instead I browse ASOS and think about getting a fringe. At 6 p.m., which is when our day is supposed to finish, I stand around making noises about being 'kind of done' until people start telling me I should leave.

7.30 p.m.

I take ballet class every week. A woman on the other side of the barre gets there later than me and then asserts herself so I have to move up, out of the spot I arrived early to claim. I am fuming about this. Then a woman on the barre behind me starts saying all of the steps loud enough for me to hear them. This would be bad enough, but she's saying them wrong, so I'm thrown off. I give her a meaningful look, which she either misses or ignores.

Halfway through the class we put the barres away. I drag one of them with some other women, but when we try to put it against the wall my thumb gets trapped. I stifle a yelp because I don't want anyone to feel bad.

Finally, when we're dancing in the centre, a woman keeps standing directly in front of me so I can't see my feet in the mirror. Every time I move, she moves too. Eventually I make a noise a bit like a sigh and she seems to notice. She moves slightly left and I can now see one of my feet. I feel painfully guilty.

9 p.m.
I'm home from ballet and I need to wash my hair, but my husband hasn't made dinner (he's not one of life's cooks – and he does all the washing-up), so I end up roasting aubergines and planning to get up earlier and wash my hair tomorrow, which will inevitably mean I am late.

11 p.m.
I'm just falling asleep as my husband starts to snore like a buzz saw. I consider sleeping elsewhere, but then decide sleeping apart means I am a bad wife. Rather than waking him up I wait until I'm seething with anger and exhaustion, then I snap and pull the duvet off him. He wakes up looking hurt and sad. I feel hideously guilty and apologise. He goes back to sleep. I listen to him snore.

No one likes homework. But in order to get the most out of this book, I would encourage you to keep a diary for a week, and to be completely honest with yourself about each moment during the day when you avoid doing something because you don't want to be rude.

RUDE: DEFINITION

ADJECTIVE. Offensively impolite or bad-mannered.
(Concise Oxford Dictionary)

December 2018
It's just before 7 a.m. and I'm standing in a TV studio, about to go on breakfast television. This is normal – this is part of my job. As a journalist and feminist commentator, I'm regularly offered a seat at a desk or on a sofa in order to, put bluntly, have a row with Piers Morgan.

The format is almost always the same. I arrive at the studio, often still half asleep, get my hair and make-up done, which functions like a kind of armour, and neck a cup of coffee. After an extensive and nuanced research chat, I then go on set and have a much less nuanced and much angrier debate with someone who has been cast because they have the exact opposite opinion to mine. I'll usually have Piers Morgan shouting from one side and a fellow panellist shouting from the other.

Today I'm nervous. The person who is attaching a microphone to my bra has cold hands. Incidentally, microphones – they go in your jacket pocket if you're a man, but if you wear a dress on TV that means you're getting a cold hand down your back while an embarrassed sound technician tries to make the mic pack clip onto your underwear.

I don't usually get nervous, but today I'm tired and stressed. It's early in the morning and I've gained a little weight in the run-up to Christmas, which means there'll be even more horrible comments on social media as soon as we're done. Plus, it's a divisive topic: should there be limits on what jokes comedians can make?

The producers shepherd me down a corridor and introduce me to my fellow guest, a comedian who was told he couldn't make sexist or racist jokes at a charity event and caused a small news story by objecting to it. 'Hi,' I smile, offering my hand. 'It's nice to meet you.' He smiles back, perfectly friendly, just as they always are.

TV producers like to keep debate guests in different rooms before the show. They do this for two reasons: because they don't want you to get into the debate off-camera, and because it's much harder to have a fiery debate with someone if you've made friends in the green room.

Anyway, they point us in the right direction and tell the comedian to stand in front of me. 'Shouldn't it be ladies first?' he smirks. 'Oh wait, is that sexist?'

I smile, perhaps roll my eyes a little, but say nothing. He is trying to wind me up. It works, but I don't acknowledge it. You see, I'm a nice girl. I don't rise to it when people try to bait me with lazy jokes about sexism. I'm here for a debate but I still want everyone to like me. This – I realise a few moments later – has always been my mistake.

Soon we're on air and I'm asked a question. The comedian has already had his say, and now he's trying to talk over me. Without thinking about it, I put my finger to my lips and I shush him, like I would if he were a naughty child. I keep shushing him, and when he continues talking I say: 'Either I can talk, or we can both talk, but I'm not going to stop talking.' And he stops.

For the first time in as long as I can remember a man has stopped talking to let me have my say. And it feels incredible, like I've shattered my own personal glass ceiling. After years of fighting to be heard at dinner parties and work meetings, I have finally snapped and thrown my full force at the problem.

The interview finishes and we make friendly noises towards each other, shake hands and part amicably. Then everything explodes. Social media lights up with horror at my behaviour. I am dubbed 'Rebecca Rude'. I am briefly a news story. I go home for Christmas and distant family members think it's funny to put their finger to their mouth and shush me as a greeting (it is quite funny, actually). Overnight I have become known as A Rude Woman.

Initially, I'm mortified. I am not rude. At least, not in the most traditional sense. I've been complimented on my manners since I was a small child. I always say 'please' and 'thank you'. I tip, I send birthday cards, I don't complain about splitting the bill even if I only had a main course. I used to write a column about etiquette and I pen a *stonking* thank-you letter.

But the longer it goes on, the more people call me 'Rebecca Rude', the more I start to realise: the last decade of my life has been a journey to de-program myself. A mission to unlearn the messages I was taught as a child and teenager. With every year that passes, I get ruder. And it is no coincidence that the ruder I get, the happier and more successful I become.

Rudeness, I realise, is a talent. And, rather than shy away from it, I'm going to turn it into my own personal superpower; you can do the exact same thing.

What does it really mean to be rude?

If we're going to talk about rudeness for the duration of an entire book, then we should understand each other; specifically, we should understand what we mean by rudeness.

There are two types of rudeness: the kind which is unacceptable, and the kind which is admirable. The best way to explain the difference is to imagine you're in a restaurant. It's the right kind of rude to let a member of staff know if your food is cold. It's the wrong kind of rude to act as if it's their fault. It's the right kind of rude to ask politely if there's another table you can move to if yours is in a draught or uncomfortably close to someone else's. It's the wrong kind of rude to be aggressive or offensive to a member of staff who isn't able to help with your request.

The kind of rudeness that this book defends is what I'd term 'positive rudeness'. It is, to be totally honest, the kind of behaviour which is called 'rude' when it comes from a woman but 'assertive' when it comes from a man. Positive rudeness means politely saying you'd prefer not to pay for any items of food which were inedible. Plain old-fashioned (unacceptable) rudeness means insulting the chef or taking out your rage on the waiting staff, who are probably tired, bored, on minimum wage and had nothing to do with the preparation of said food.

Some rude behaviour is not admirable, or even defensible. Snapping your fingers at a waitress or waiter is not OK. Shouting across the room to get service, making snide comments about the staff, looking down your nose at fellow diners or loudly insulting the food all fall within the category of unacceptably rude. It's never going to be OK deliberately to upset someone, to call another person a name. If you're looking for a book which defends that kind of rudeness then you are, to coin a phrase, shit out of luck here. This book is going to show you what life looks like when you stop worrying that you might seem rude.

It's not (always) easy, being rude

I won't lie: on my path towards rebalancing the levels of rudeness that I deploy day to day, I have sometimes got it wrong. Having spent my entire life trying to avoid being rude, it was a challenge to call upon the right amount of it at the right time. Take, for example, my rude epiphany on national breakfast television. Just after the 'shushing' I said, 'You've had your chance to speak and now I am going to have mine.' A sentence which every woman should become used to saying, because it's an essential statement to be able to make in modern life. But no one was particularly interested in that part: what people cared about was the shush, which was possibly a little bit childish. It felt good though.

Attempting to create the perfect cocktail of rude has been a challenge. Sometimes I have sent an email to someone senior to me which was too rude. Honest, accurate and probably fair, but not the most efficient way to get the reaction I wanted. Similarly, I have approached debates at parties with a ferocity more appropriate for a boardroom takeover than for drinks with mates. Skewering a friend of a friend's boyfriend because he gets the numbers wrong when he cites the 2017 election might win the argument, but it doesn't win you any friends.

Plus, being rude goes against all of my natural urges. When a taxi driver shouted at me at the end of a journey (I still don't understand why), I gave him the finger and reported him to the app I had hired him from. But then, rather than being pleased that I'd prevented him from shouting at other women, I spent several days feeling guilty for overreacting. Maybe he'd had a hard day? Maybe he didn't realise that shouting at me was wrong? Having spent so much of my life assuming that my feelings were either wrong or secondary to those of others, rewriting the rules felt uncomfortable as hell.

I've encountered a whole lot of self-help books in my time which generally propose that they can fix your life with a few simple and easy steps. I cannot do that. All I can do is give you the tools with which to redress the balance.

Why does rudeness matter?

Of all the things in the world to worry about, why would anyone put the right for women to be rude at the top of the list?

It's a fair question. Happily, there is a very simple answer: because I believe that an inability to be rude is one of the biggest issues which still inhibits the equality of women today. When I was twenty-two I worked as a receptionist for a PR firm in central London. Every day I got the Tube from my huge shared house to the office. One morning, while squashed into a packed carriage, I realised that someone had put their hand up my skirt. My initial reaction was mortification. I'd put my arse on some poor person's hand. So I moved. And of course, the hand moved with me.

I stood for three stops, trying to work out whether the groping was deliberate. I was so scared that I would wrongly accuse one of the people rammed in behind me of touching me up that I said nothing.

Eventually it became very clear that this was a determined attempt at getting under my tights. I wriggled away without so much a backwards glance, and spent the whole day feeling wretched. I've heard dozens of women tell the same story. 'I wasn't sure if he was doing it on purpose,' 'I didn't want to assume,' 'I thought it might have been an accident.' The fear of being so 'arrogant' or 'up yourself' that you think a man would want to touch you and then being proven wrong is enough to create silence – to allow someone to try to get into your knickers on a public train. In 2018 there were 1,206 recorded incidents of women being sexually assaulted on the London Underground network. However, campaigners believe that the crime, which is often committed by people who deliberately take the Tube in order to harass or assault, is under-reported. And honestly, I'm not surprised.

There have been other times when I've been on busy public transport and I've been unsure whether or not the touching was deliberate. Does that man mean to have his hand on my hip, my chest or my buttock? Or is it just a busy train? Time and time again I have placed the fear of offending him, of making him feel embarrassed, above my own need to take the Tube without having hands in places which make me feel uncomfortable.

Women aren't only putting up with being harassed or assaulted out of politeness. They're also having ostensibly consensual sex for the same reason.

I had always assumed that I was the only woman who could possibly be so flaccid in her resolution that she would have sex to avoid giving offence. But, in the course of writing my article, I realised that this wasn't at all true. Maya, a twenty-eight-year-old personal trainer, told me:

I'm pretty sure that the majority of my sexual experiences in my teens and twenties were done out of politeness. You end up in a situation where you're worried about offending someone if you don't go ahead – whether you've led them on or what they'll think about themselves if you back out at the last minute. And, in relationships, I've had sex when I definitely did not want to but just kind of felt bad about not doing it – what if the other person thought that I thought they were crap in bed or didn't fancy them anymore?

In day-to-day life Maya is a ballsy, smart, powerful woman with whom you'd be nervous to get into a debate.

After I wrote the article, I got more emails than I could keep track of from women just like me, and just like Maya, who considered themselves confident and powerful, smart and impressive, but who had done the exact same thing. Had sex entirely out of politeness.

The funny thing about being rude, or having a fear of it, is that once you start cataloguing the things you have or have not done in order not to seem rude the list starts to spiral. To every man I've ever turned down in a bar I have said that I have a boyfriend, because I didn't want to be rude. Each time I've hassled a commissioning editor for a fee that I'm owed I have started the email with, 'I am so sorry, I know you must be terribly busy,' because I didn't want to be rude. I've donated money to charity, attended dreadful parties, eaten things that made me feel sick and lent things I knew I'd never get back. All because I didn't want to be rude. And I guarantee that if you make a list of everything you've done lately that you didn't want to do, the motive will have been not to appear rude.

At the lighter end of the spectrum, my fear of rudeness has got me some terrible nights out, stretched clothing returned by taller friends and horrible meals. At the darker end are sexual encounters I'd pay money to forget and terrifying lifts with drunk drivers. Whenever you go to a party you're dreading, full of horrible people, watch someone else get a promotion that you deserved, or don't shout your head off when someone touches you up on the Tube, it is all too easy to become a victim of your own politeness. Sometimes the only way to escape a situation is to be rude. That is why rudeness matters.

In order to write this book, I needed to hear about other people's experiences of rudeness. The best thing about the interviews I did, the anecdotes I scribbled down on my phone on the Tube or in the pub, and the questionnaire that hundreds of people filled out online was realising that other women had done the same things I had. The only difference was that I was able to be kind to these women in a way that I couldn't be kind to myself. While internally I called myself weak and spineless for having allowed men to have sex with me in order to avoid the embarrassment of saying no, I was willing to cut every other woman I spoke to a huge amount of slack. 'Of course you didn't feel you could say no,' I listened to myself say to one woman as I transcribed our interview. 'We've been brought up to make other people happy, to say yes whenever possible.'

I learned in that moment that the only person I had never had any trouble being rude to was myself. In any given day I would call myself stupid, fat, lazy, useless, boring, repetitive, fraudulent and any number of other horrible words – things that I would never say to another person, not someone I disliked, let alone someone I loved. I resolved to try – and continue to try – to treat myself in the same way that I treat my friends. Part of redressing my rudeness levels meant that I had to take my inner rudeness down from a 100 to a 10 (I often need a self-pep talk to get up in the morning, and I require stern self-talking-tos about the state of my bedroom).

A brief history of rude

Before we can break the cycle of being afraid to be rude, we need to understand where it comes from. For most of us, the fear of being regarded as rude starts in childhood.

I realise that starting with childhood isn't exactly revolutionary. But it's true. Our parents spend hours and hours trying to drill into us that we have to ask to leave the table when we've finished our food, wait quietly to speak, put our hands up in class, bless people when they sneeze and cover our mouths when we yawn. Now, some of this I'm on board with. When I worked as a nanny I was an absolute stickler for saying please and thank you. It might sound counter-intuitive, but I firmly believe that you can be rude while still having lovely manners.

I draw a line between the kind of politeness which costs you nothing and helps others – saying please and thank you, saying good morning to a receptionist or a doorman – and that which *The Power of Rude* should help you rebalance, specifically the kind of politeness which makes you think that your own needs, wants and opinions are less important than those of the people around you.

Much of what we are taught when we're kids is about self-sacrifice. Your friend wants to play with your toy? Hand it over. There's only one sweetie left? Give it to your sister. And while the intention is to create selfless, self-sacrificing adults, what it often does is breed adults who believe that their own wants and needs should come at the absolute bottom of the pile, leaving them unable to be pushy or demanding when they need to be. A friend's Australian husband recently remarked that he loves eating dinner with Brits because they all pretend that they don't want the last potato.

He doesn't take part in this charade, and therefore always gets to eat it.

Little girls, I'm afraid to say, have it worse than boys. Just look at the nineteenth-century poem, thought to have been written by Robert Southey, which most of us will have heard on the playground or in nursery school:

> What are little boys made of?
> What are little boys made of?
> Slugs and snails
> And puppy-dogs' tails.
> That's what little boys are made of.
>
> What are little girls made of?
> What are little girls made of?
> Sugar and spice
> And all things nice.
> That's what little girls are made of.

Gender-neutral parenting might be fashionable these days, but if you were born more than ten years ago and your parents weren't advanced gender scholars the chances are you had a gendered childhood. That doesn't mean that you were forbidden from wearing blue or told that you weren't allowed to like football. Gender stereotyping is more insidious than that.

Your parents probably didn't mean to treat you differently from your brothers or any other little boys in your social group. But I'll bet they still did. There are too many inherited stereotypes without any scientific basis not to. 'Boys will be boys,' boys mature more slowly than girls, boys are naturally aggressive, boys need an outlet for their energy. None of it is true, but that doesn't mean that you managed to avoid a childhood in which you were forced to sit on your hands and wait nicely while boys were allowed to run around outside to 'burn off their energy'.

A 2018 study by First News found that the majority of children aged between nine and fourteen felt that they were treated differently because of their gender. One ten-year-old even commented that she had been told at school that she needed to be more 'ladylike'. Rudeness is the absolute opposite of being 'ladylike'. In fact, The Power of Rude throws a full martini in the face of 'ladylike' and then sleeps with its husband. Being 'ladylike' is about being sweet, quiet, unprovocative and allowing life to happen around you while you put out more finger sandwiches. Being rude is about grabbing the world by the balls and twisting until you get what you want.

One of the most frustrating lines that children are subjected to is the oft-repeated claim that 'girls mature more quickly than boys'. According to clinical psychologist Dr Hamira Ruiz, this is not proven. She explains: 'While it is true that neuroscientists are making new discoveries about how the brain rewires itself during/after puberty and there is some MRI evidence to suggest that the adolescent female brain prunes itself differently and at a faster pace compared to the male brain, it is still a very big leap of inference to link neuronal changes in the brain to gender-specific behaviours.' But, while the research suggests that boys do not develop more slowly, the expectation that they will do so often becomes a self-fulfilling prophecy. Girls are held to a higher standard and made responsible for their actions from an earlier age, which means that we start thinking about – and worrying about – being rude while our brains are at their most elastic.

'Boys will be boys' is another one of those catch-all expressions that used to be prevalent. Thankfully, modern-day parents seem to be eschewing it as an excuse, but it's still an ingrained attitude. When I was a nanny I spent many hours sitting on the edge of a playground and, thanks to my dodgy iPhone battery, I often didn't have anything to do but watch the children play. If you ever find yourself in the same situation, observe how childcare providers treat boys and girls differently. Girls are told far more frequently to let other children have a go on the swings, slide or whatever the most interesting bit of the playground is.

There is an enduring perception that boys have more energy and mature more slowly, therefore they need to be allowed to run around, climb on furniture, interrupt their parents' conversations and generally be ruder. Girls, on the other hand, have this behaviour stamped out of them far earlier.

Is it any wonder, given that we're indoctrinated from our early childhood, that by the time we reach adulthood we women struggle to be assertive in the workplace? As Dr Riaz confirmed to me in an interview, the messages that we're given about gender and expectation while we're children are pretty hardwired by adulthood:

> We know that human beings are first and foremost, social animals; this means we are hypersensitive to what's expected of us by our 'tribe', especially during adolescence, when a key psychological challenge is to arrive at a personal identity that allows us simultaneously to fit in and to stand out.
>
> If ungrounded gender stereotypes of this type are transmitted from one generation to the next without being challenged, we risk unwittingly passing on culturally redundant limiting beliefs – instead of empowering teenagers to explore their individual potential to the fullest, we are herding them into mini-cages painted pink and blue.

As little girls we are told over and over again to wait our turn, share nicely, say please and thank you and not to interrupt.

Then, as adults, we wait our turn for a promotion. We share nicely instead of grabbing the space we need. We say please when we want to speak in a meeting or around the dinner table, and we say thank you when we're permitted the space to speak. We don't interrupt to ask for pay rises and we don't complain if we don't get them. We stay quiet when men put their hands up our skirts on public transport because we don't want to make a fuss. We say to men in bars that we don't want to have a drink with them because we have boyfriends, rather than telling the truth: that we don't want to.

As children, we are rewarded for being quiet, for being self-contained, for getting on with things silently and for not making a fuss. We are encouraged to play nicely, not to take up space or make noise. Our parents are pleased if we don't draw attention to ourselves. We are rewarded for all of these traits. Until adulthood, when suddenly the ability to push yourself forward becomes the hallmark of success. In short, while trying to teach us not to be rude, our parents program us to be the architects of our own oppression. The lessons that we are taught as little girls are the very same ones which oppress us when we grow up. As Dr Riaz says, we are trapped in cages of pink and blue. And, at least as far as I am concerned, the bars of those pink cages are our fear of being rude.

CHAPTER ONE

RUDE TO YOUR FRIENDS

The famous thinker Albus Dumbledore (Order of Merlin, first class) once said: 'It takes a great deal of bravery to stand up to our enemies, but just as much to stand up to our friends.' Only, of course, it was J.K. Rowling who wrote those words, and she had a bloody good point: being rude to people you'll never see again is one thing, not always easy, but possible; being rude to those who have known you for your entire life, and who have come to expect a certain type of behaviour from you, is much harder. But our friends are some of the people we spend most of our time with and are also most likely to ask things of us, so they're actually some of the most important ones to learn to be rude to.

When I was thirteen, the film *Mean Girls* came out. If you haven't seen it, put this book down and go and watch it because, honestly, it's the greatest cinematic triumph of all time and still deserves a retrospective Oscar nomination for Best Picture. For those who saw it in 2004 and not since, a brief refresher: Cady Heron moves back to the US from Africa (the part of Africa is never made explicitly clear) having been home-schooled. She's never experienced Western teenagers before, and quickly learns that Girl World is a complicated, self-governing cosmos within itself. The astonishing thing about the film is that the observations it makes about female friendships were as true of my friends at an all-girl school in East Sussex as they are about teenagers at a fictional high school in Michigan. No matter where you live, the ability to say, 'I love your skirt' to a person's face and then, seconds later, behind her back, 'That is the ugliest effing skirt I've ever seen' remains true.

The cruelty that we inflicted upon each other as teenagers was beyond shocking. I made up rumours about girls in our year sucking their own nipples, masturbating with Parker fountain pens and having affairs with their riding instructors, because my ability to tell a good story made me worth having around. I peer-pressured, bullied, gossiped, bitched and hurt the young women around me, and in turn had all of those things done to me. All of it sneaky, all of it silent, all of it underhand. And while I thought of this as a teenage tendency, I noticed into my twenties that some of it was still going on.

Romantically we behave – or at least try to behave – completely differently as adults from the way we did as teenagers. We don't call men and hang up over and over again, or make up and break up three times in the same day. We don't tell our friends every minute detail of our sexual progress towards penetration and we don't let our mates decide whether we have feelings for someone or not. I noticed at about the time I left university that, while my attitude to men and sex had changed as I'd got older, much of my behaviour towards my friends (mainly talking about them behind their backs and worrying that they all hated me) was just as it had been when I was a teenager, the only real difference being that we were now doing it over wine in our own flats rather than Diet Coke in our parents' houses.

Friendship is a complex, tricky area which many of us struggle to navigate, but if you (like me) have sleepwalked into your twenties or thirties, still handling your friendships in the same way you did in your teens, then it might be time to have a think about what needs to change.

Bitching, aggression and anger

It's a bit of a generalisation that male friendships and female friendships are inherently different, but anecdotally it seems to be true. Men and boys are more inclined towards telling their friends if they are annoyed with them, perhaps resorting to physical violence (undoubtedly true when they are children) and then making up again. Women and girls are much less likely to hit each other. Perhaps some of that is down to testosterone, but it's certainly true that violence isn't expected of us as women. But it doesn't mean that we skip the fight. All it means is that instead of fighting with our fists we fight with words, and even that has to be underhand and sneaky because it's essential to keep a pretty face on at all times.

There is a tendency with modern feminism to blame the patriarchy for anything and everything, which can seem a little lazy, but when you unpack the accusation it turns out often to be true. I don't want to blame 'society' for the fact that women are horrible about their friends, but realistically there is an element of truth to it. The pressure for women always to seem nice and be sweet-natured peacemakers is an impossible burden to bear. So, in order to try to live up to that expectation, we avoid conflict with our friends by talking about them behind their backs.

Standing up to your male friends is (from what I've observed) often as simple as saying, 'Fuck off mate.' If I told one of my friends to fuck off the entire conversation would grind to a halt and everyone would ask why I was being so aggressive. When one of my girlfriends upsets me, the temptation is to either say nothing, or to say nothing and then complain about it to someone else. Taking it to a confrontation would probably mean going out for a drink and having a calm, measured discussion about how we had upset each other. I cannot imagine anything less likely than a physical brawl between me and one of my friends.

Usually, using words to try to explain things rather than saying 'Fuck off' or throwing a punch is the better way to go about it, but in the case of conflict women get a raw deal. We have to play nice, so we rarely enjoy the catharsis of really blowing up at a friend. And because we're not allowed to have the row, we end up bitching about each other. Sadly, we all know that if someone will bitch with you, they'll bitch about you, which means that any friend with whom you enjoy a good gossip is probably doing the exact same thing to you when your back is turned.

In *Mean Girls*, Cady Heron acknowledges that girls channel aggression into verbal sparring instead of physicality, saying, 'This was Girl World, and in Girl World all the fighting had to be sneaky' – a theory which is consistent with behavioural studies of women, especially teenage girls.

According to a 2013 UN study on drugs and crime, 'globally, men are more violent than women'. However, as reported in a study titled *An Integrated Review of Indirect, Relational, and Social Aggression* by Richardson, Archer and Coyne (2005), women frequently engage in other forms of aggressive behaviour, and use indirect aggression to an equivalent or greater extent than men. Indirect aggression includes spreading false rumours, gossiping, excluding people from social groups, making insinuations and criticising others' appearance or personality, all of which sounds very familiar. Archer's study found that girls' use of indirect aggression exceeded that of boys from the age of eleven onwards, and that this difference persisted into adulthood.

And then social norms and expectations come into play, because most cultures endorse warfare as a means to gain status and are patriarchal, so they reward men for being warriors but punish women for being aggressive.

Something that struck me about this research is that it seems to suggest that it's normal for people to need somewhere to put their anger. I've noticed that often, when I've been angered by an experience – being pushed on public transport, someone making a sharp comment during a meeting, a friend cancelling at the last minute when I've already left the house – I have been unable to shake the inner frustration which hangs around afterwards. It's not just towards strangers, either. Often, I will bite my tongue during an argument, or delete the frustrated WhatsApp message that I wanted to send a friend, but that anger doesn't just magically disappear. Without a place to put it, it festers. I will find myself still raging about a relatively minor incident which happened a week ago, because I didn't allow my frustration any breathing room at the time.

While I would never condone starting fights with strangers on the Tube or giving in to every impulse of anger that you feel, allowing your anger some oxygen is genuinely important. By saying, 'Excuse me, that hurt' to the person who shoved you out of the way to get on the train, or 'I'm frustrated that you told me you would take the bins out but didn't', you remove the anger from your internal pressure cooker, which means you can move on.

Groups and break-ups

The idea that women have neat little circles of female friends, all of whom adore each other, is something of a fiction. If you do have a group of girlfriends who live close together, are all equally close to each other, and spend time doing activities and talking about their lives and never get sick of each other, then you are a) killing it and b) living in a TV show directed by Darren Star.

The far, far more common way to have friendships is through a hotchpotch of different people from different stages of your life, all of whom are familiar with each other but mostly via you. It's also extremely likely that there will be a few people in your extended social circle whom you don't especially like, but whom you keep in your life because they're part of the group and it would be more work to get rid of them than it is to pretend to care when they talk about their boyfriend/cat/job/ craft projects. It's fine not to love everyone in your social circle equally, but when you get to the stage when you are spending precious hours of your life humouring someone who doesn't really like you, whom you really don't enjoy being with, you have got to ask why. If the answer is 'Because I don't know how not to', then you've got some thinking to do.

We all know how to break up with a romantic partner. We've been reading about it since before we were old enough to date, and watching it on TV and in films. The guidelines are easy to follow – you're supposed to be honest, do it in person and expect to feel sad afterwards. After a while of wallowing, crying and listening to Taylor Swift you take up kick-boxing, get a haircut and – bam – you're a brand-new woman. I'm being a little facetious, perhaps, but there is a routine and a ritual to a romantic break-up; it's almost like a sacrament. But we don't have anything of the sort when it comes to friendship break-ups. In fact, even having a friendship break-up is unusual.

When I was a teenager, a friend and I decided to break up. We went out to lunch at Pizza Express (the height of sophistication), had an afternoon of shopping in town (aka sitting on a bench in the mall) and then agreed that that was it: when we went back to school after the holidays we would be broken up and would focus on other friendships. It was a bit cringe worthy and dramatic, as befits teenage girls, but the central thesis was actually pretty solid. Admittedly, it was probably motivated by the fact that we went to an all-girls school, so didn't know any boys but wanted to experience a break-up. But there was a sound sentiment at the core of it. We had ceased to be good friends to each other so we decided to bring the relationship to a close, something which most people seem reticent to do in platonic relationships even if they would happily do so in a romantic one. When it comes to dumping a romantic partner, women are able to supersede the rudeness of rejecting someone because the framework is well established. We have societal permission to do so, as long as there is a 'good' reason (of course, you shouldn't need any reason other than not being happy in the relationship).

Because friendship break-ups are uncommon, we have not developed a language and routine around how to handle them. It doesn't occur to us that we're allowed to say, 'Thanks but no thanks' to the women in our lives, so we limp along, going out for drinks with people who undermine and belittle us, or spending weekends staying with people who live on the other side of the country and talk exclusively about themselves the entire time.

I've been dumped by a friend as an adult and it was the

most traumatic break-up I've ever had. We had been extremely close for five or six years, but I had changed a great deal in that time. She was older, established and settled in her life, whereas I had gone from student to receptionist to writer, and from single to engaged over the course of our friendship. Initially I chalked up her rejection to an inability to cope with my changing fortunes. The dynamic on which our friendship was based was that she was the older, wiser and dominant friend; I was the sillier, younger and sweeter one who did whatever she wanted whenever she wanted. For a while it worked – I liked having someone who organised my social life for me, who could advise me on the best course of action and generally be a sort of demi-mother figure, but as I got older and more independent I started to feel suffocated and patronised.

Eventually we had a fight and she blocked me on all methods of communication, as was her right. At the time I was devastated, but now I admire her for doing it. Unlike me – I cling to every friend I have lest I one day find myself unable to fill a Saturday night with plans – she was bold (rude) enough to decide she no longer wanted anything to do with me. In the long run, by doing the rude thing she saved us both a lot of strained lunches, passive-aggressive WhatsApps and resentful dinner parties.

'I just don't get on with girls'

There are two sentences that set my teeth on edge. Actually, there are a lot of sentences that set my teeth on edge, but at the forefront of the teeth-setting are 'I don't really get on with girls' and 'I find that other women are very jealous of me.' During the 2019 series of UK *Love Island*, Lucie Donlan hit the headlines for telling fellow contestants that she didn't hang out with other women. When asked why she was acting in a withdrawn manner, she told fellow contestants, 'It's because I hang out with guys when I'm at home, I don't hang out with girls.' She then went on to say, 'I've never had a girlfriend. Never. All guys, always.' Justifying this stance, she said that she preferred men because they 'tell it how it is' whereas 'girls are drama'.

The perception that women are more complicated than men and therefore harder work is best described as internalised misogyny. Internalised misogyny is quite a highfalutin feminist expression, but it's a way of explaining that women who live with sexism can often absorb that sexism and end up perpetuating it. It's not your fault that you might on some level think that women are less good at driving than men – you've grown up in a world which claims that is the truth (NB: women get into fewer traffic accidents than men do), and you think this way because of internalised misogyny.

For a long time, I felt that I had to try to convince women who said that they didn't want girlfriends that they really did, deep down. My people-pleasing personality extended to trying to persuade people who had said outright that they did not want to be my friend that they should be my friend. Over the last couple of years, as my friendship groups have shrunk in the way they so often do as you approach thirty, I have stopped bothering with that tendency. If someone is dumb enough to eschew the magic of female friendship because she's written off an entire gender, then that's fine by me. I'm going to move on, and have nothing more to say on the matter.

Introducing rudeness to your friendships

If you've always been a bit rude, then getting ruder isn't so hard. But if, like so many of us, you've either put on a nice-girl face or actually been a nice girl, then it's difficult to change that overnight. If you go from picking up other people's dry cleaning to turning down your best mate's thirtieth-birthday dinner because you'd rather stay home and watch *One Tree Hill* repeats, that's going to cause problems in your life.

The obvious option is to go softly-softly. Slowly introduce a little bit of straight talking and then, in about a decade, you'll be able to skip a girls' night on the other side of town being held at a raw vegan restaurant. But the problem there is that it doesn't really fit with the whole power of rude philosophy, does it?

The best way to introduce rudeness into your friendship is to make it mutual. It might be hurtful to think about, but the truth is: your friends want to cancel on you just as often as you want to cancel on them. Your heart might sink at the idea of sitting outside a rammed pub in central London watching them down glasses of wine, but they may well have the same reaction when you push for a 9 a.m. Sunday morning run and brunch. Bringing the power of rude into your friendship isn't about you being the arbiter of everything. It's about saying to the people you love, 'I don't think that we should do things that make us stressed or unhappy any more. I'm going to start by telling you when I don't want to do something, or when I'm too tired or broke. And I'd really like you to do the same thing.'

The power of rude isn't just about getting you out of doing things you don't want to do, it's about getting you to make an informed choice about how much of that stuff you are going to do. It's never going to be OK to become totally selfish and only ever spend time on what you feel like doing – you're going to be very fat, poor and unemployed if that's the case – but it's about being honest with yourself and other people and making a sensible assessment of each and every situation. Going to visit your grandparents? Important. Going to an expensive group meal with people you don't really know? Pointless.

My younger sister has an expression: 'That sounds really nice, I don't want to come.' It's a silly, flippant turn of phrase, but it works. When I have tickets to a stand-up show five minutes from my house, which means she has to travel two hours, she says it. When I try to convince her that she will enjoy coming to my adult ballet class? Same thing. An activity which will thrill you might well leave me cold, and I don't have to pretend otherwise.

Of course, in life, to a certain extent, all of us have to do things which we don't want to do. Most of the time the parties that we're dreading end up being the ones where we have the most fun; but by the same token, if you know you're not willing or able to attend a social event, you should be able to be honest about it rather than lying at the last moment, which, as I've said before, is the wrong kind of rude.

Before writing *The Power of Rude*, my friendships were without a doubt the aspect of my life where I most needed to take my own medicine. A close friend had taken to inserting her child into every conversation, making her the focal point, and also physically bringing her along without warning me that she was going to. On evenings when I wanted to smoke a cigarette, drink a large glass of wine and swear at will, I had to sit in her living room and admire how clever her small child was for picking up wooden blocks. So I told her, face to face – not over WhatsApp, as I wanted to. I said something along the lines of (and of course this is more polished and peppered with the word 'like' than it was in real life): 'I really love Luna,* and I would like to spend time with her, but I feel like we don't talk about much else any more and, as a non-parent, I don't find conversations about her development terribly stimulating. I've got very little to add. Can we try to have some adult-only time, and maybe talk about you rather than your child?'

Initially it didn't go down well. She cried. But that was as much about the shock of this level of honesty as anything else. Then she told me something along the lines of (again, polished and the crying taken out): 'I don't think you're interested in my daughter, who is the focal point of my life. Becoming a mum has been incredibly hard and, whether you are interested or not, you have an obligation as my friend to listen to me talk about things that are significant to me. I'm sorry that I'm not the friend you had before I had kids, but I'm not the same person any more.'

Eventually, after a glass of wine, we came to a compromise: we would split our time together between me coming over, seeing both my friend and her child, and going out together like we used to. Since then, our friendship has been noticeably closer and more robust, and the way in which we speak to each other has become more genuine. Initially, I think she felt that I was being rude because I didn't care, but in reality the only reason I did it was because I value her so much.

Bringing the power of rude into your friendship will, almost certainly, create work. You'll need to explain and explore what it is that you want to change. It might sound counter-intuitive, but being rude to your friends really can be an act of love.

---

* Name changed because I'm rude, but I'm not stupid, and I'd really like to still be her friend.

Boundaries

In 2019, an academic named Melissa A. Fabello briefly became Internet-famous after she suggested sending friends a sort of 'out of office' message if they got in touch looking for emotional support at a time when you weren't in a position to give it. She tweeted:

> I am the kind of person who people reach out to when they're in pain. Because I'm good at emotional processing *and* logical problem-solving, I tend to be a go-to for my friends who need to externally process their experiences. Too often, friends unload on me without warning – which not only interrupts whatever I'm working on or going through, but also throws me into a stressful state of crisis mode that is hard to come down from. Unless it is *truly* an emergency, that's unfair.

Initially I found myself irritated by Fabello's comments, but I tried to examine the reason for my annoyance, and when I audited my frustration I found that it stemmed from a rejection of her highly therapised way of speaking and my ingrained rejection of anyone who wants to put themselves first.

In reality, I understand Fabello's predicament: I'm also someone to whom people come if they need to talk; I'm a decent listener, I'm generally interested in other people's problems and I will always have wine in the house. Perhaps, I realised, as I read more about Fabello's theory, my anger at her way of handling needy friends was more because I had always assumed that it was compulsory to drop everything and listen to someone else's issues on demand.

Fabello then suggested a template for responding to someone who has asked for your support at an inconvenient time. The template reads: 'Hey! I'm so glad you reached out. I'm actually at capacity dealing with someone else who's in crisis/dealing with some personal stuff right now and I don't think I can hold appropriate space for you. Could we connect at [later date or time] instead?/Do you have someone else you can reach out to?' Again, when I first read it I bristled, deciding that this was the absolute zenith of modern selfishness. Given the barrage of replies, it was clear that Fabello had stumbled on something real – that it's true that we should put the needs of others before our own sometimes, but also that it is perfectly valid to tell someone you don't have room to hear about their horrible boyfriend for the fifteenth time.

While it might seem cruel and cold to tell someone that you're not in the mood to listen, it is OK to need space and not to have the bandwidth to help someone out at any time of the day or night. Emergencies are emergencies, and therefore an entirely separate thing. But, in terms of your average low-level request for support, boundaries are legitimate (however New Age Goop that might sound). If, for the people you love, you set the expectation that they will have your support only when it can be given freely and without resentment, they might actually end up feeling more able to turn to you than not.

Is it rude to tell your friend that you don't have the emotional energy to spend on them? Probably, a bit, yes. Is it the right kind of rude? Probably, also yes, depending on your reciprocal expectations. If you send a friendship 'out of office', you need to be prepared to get one back.

Babies and friendships

One of the biggest hurdles any of us face in long-term friendships is that, at some point, one of you will probably decide to move the goalposts by procreating. Suddenly, when you become a parent, all bets are off. Having a baby lobs a rock into the millpond of your friendship and the ripples extend far beyond you and your partner. Don't get me wrong, becoming a parent is a miracle; however, it's also something that you choose for yourself but impose on everyone else in your life. I don't have children, but lots of my friends do, and I've seen first-hand how it unavoidably changes your relationships with them. However hard you try, there is a line between people with young children and people without them, and it's a line which makes the power of rude very complicated.

Let's take a classic (and real) dilemma: a woman who recently had a baby is due to go to a friend's birthday dinner in a few weeks' time. Her baby, who is exclusively breast-fed and therefore cannot be left for the duration of the dinner, is three months old. She wants to bring the baby to the dinner – it will probably sleep through most of it – but her friend, who does not have children and is planning a big boozy night, does not want the baby to come because it will 'change the dynamic', and if she says yes to one baby, other people might want to bring their kids as well.

It's a perfect example because no one is right and no one is wrong. The birthday girl doesn't want to be sitting in the middle of an NCT group wearing a sparkly dress which someone's darling little angel eventually voms on, but the friend doesn't want to become a social pariah because her baby – who probably, being asleep, would not distract from the party – cannot be left at home.

If I were advising the birthday girl to be rude, I would tell her to pull rank: it's her birthday, so she makes the rules and she wants a child-free evening, therefore she is entitled to have that. Were I advising the new mum, I would tell her that she has every right to ask her friends to make reasonable adjustments to include her, and that if they're not willing to have the baby at the party then sadly she won't be able to come. At the end of the day, all you can really do is try to be both rude and kind. Being rude does not mean suspending your humanity or your sense of decency.

In real life, the situation was (somewhat) solved by the mum attending just the early part of the dinner while her partner looked after the baby nearby. The birthday girl and the friend group made a huge fuss of the new mum while she was there, and everyone came away from it feeling they had at least tried.

Unfortunately, in my experience as a person who doesn't have children, the burden tends to fall most on us. I've spent a lot of time at birthday parties or soft-play centres playing hide and seek, waiting for a friend to ask a question about me, which never comes. It is hard, and it would be disingenuous to pretend otherwise; however it's also enormously worthwhile. And, let's face it, if people stopped having babies, then the human race would come to a swift end. But it seems that much of the time the options are either to be honest or to be supportive, and there is no reason why you can't be both. Spend a Saturday morning in an aquarium with a screaming hangover and other people's kids, but be honest that you are there because you love your friend, not because you love child-centric weekend activities. And share the fact that you're delighted to do it today, but you'd really like a martini in a dark bar, just the two of you, at some point in the near future.

When a friend has a baby it's a bit like her moving to a

different part of the country, becoming teetotal or going vegan. It's a change that you didn't choose, but that you have to roll with if you want to sustain the friendship. It's OK to acknowledge that this is difficult for you, but it's also OK for your friend to take a little more from you than she gives back, as long as that is rebalanced in the long run.

One of my closest friends doesn't want children. She is resolute about this. She also says she really does not like children, full stop. I, on the other hand, very much want to grow my family one day. Said friend has always been completely clear that she is not interested in my potential offspring, and that she will not be up for the package deal. She'll be around for me when it's just me, and she'll be delighted to be the fun person I see while someone else babysits. Sometimes it makes me sad to know that our friendship will be changed if and when I have children. Occasionally I feel angry with her for not even being able to pretend that she'll be there for me when I'm a new mum, or that she'll be excited to be around for my kids, but at least her total honesty means that I know exactly what to expect. It's much better than a load of pseudo-enthusiasm followed by a wall of surprising silence when the reality of losing a friend to motherhood sets in.

'Losing' is a loaded word, it's true, but it can be exactly how the experience feels. Lola, thirty-two, tells me:

My best friend of ten years had a baby, and now she's a different person. All she talks about, thinks about, cares about is being a mum. She hasn't asked me a single question about myself in the nine months since her child was born, and it's exhausting. To start with I went over to her place, did all the washing-up, offered to take the baby – all of the stuff that you are supposed to do – but the months went on and eventually it got to the point where she was too draining to be around. I've been taking space from her and I do feel guilty, but I also feel like I deserve a friend who does give at least a bit of a shit about me.

So often, being 'rude' is less about finding a solution or actually demanding change and more about taking the lid off the pressure cooker. When you feel that you have expressed your anger, it alleviates it. Having a fight with someone who is hormonal and sleep-deprived really isn't a great move, so in navigating friendships with people who've recently had kids, I would suggest that your rude tendencies can probably wait a few months: take a step back and focus on other friends if you need to, but allow the episiotomy to heal before you start complaining about unanswered WhatsApps.

Parents vs non-parents

One of the biggest gaps that still exists between different groups in society is that between parents and non-parents. There's a wage gap between women who do and do not have children, various social settings are either devoted to serving kids or bar them entirely, and if you debate any topic long enough, someone will put on a saintly voice and say, 'As a parent . . .', as if having had a child validates their opinion above those of people who have committed to contraception.

In 2019 the *Guardian* published an anonymous letter from a child-free couple to their neighbours, who had recently had a child, which exemplified the parent/non-parent divide. It read:

My wife and I are childless through choice, but we have never judged anyone's decision to become parents. This was tested to the limit when we moved in next door to you, only a few days before your daughter was born.

Now my wife and I have some experience of what it would be like to be new parents: we know how it feels to be woken several times a night by what, at that hour, has the effect on the nerves of a fire alarm. You chose to keep your daughter in the master bedroom with you: a single layer of brick was our only protection from months of nightly screaming. Her protracted wailing cost us dozens of hours of sleep at a time when our careers were stressful and demanding. It placed an unwelcome strain on our own relationship, and soured our enjoyment of our new home.

You never apologised, or even mentioned it. I saw no evidence you ever tried to mitigate the noise for our sake, by moving her to another room, say. I've known enough new parents to know it won't have occurred to you to do so. We certainly never asked: in our child-worshipping culture, there is no more egregious social blunder than to request that a parent limit the disturbance caused by their young offspring. It's assumed that we, a childless couple, don't understand and have no right to comment.

We do understand parenthood is difficult and frustrating and, above all, exhausting. I'm sure that whatever we endured was orders of magnitude worse for you. However, as callous as this may sound, the world doesn't stop just because you've had a child. The people around you have their own lives to cope with, their own problems that they don't inflict on others. To expect them to share your discomfort is deeply selfish.

Last week I overheard you telling another neighbour that you're having a second baby. I don't expect you will show any more consideration for us than you did with your first. I just hope this one turns out to be a little quieter.

The debate about who was right and who was wrong raged online: babies do not have a volume control, some people argued; it's not fair to be unable to sleep because of someone else's choice to have a child, argued others. But the major point here isn't who is right or who is wrong, it is the total lack of communication. The people with the new baby didn't take a bottle of wine round to the neighbours to acknowledge that they had probably broken the peace by bringing a child into the house. Similarly, the neighbours didn't go round with a bunch of flowers and enquire about any soundproofing which could be arranged. Instead they sat, fuming and sleep-deprived, in their flat, letting the resentment grow.

When you allow yourself to be a little bit rude, which in this situation would have meant popping a note under the door saying, 'Congratulations on your new arrival – could we find a time to chat about sound-proofing?', you take the heat out of it. The thing that turns reasonable rude into seething anger is repressing it. When you sit on the anger for days, weeks or months you put it into a pressure cooker which heats it up into something bigger, darker and angrier which eventually takes over everything.

It is genuinely mad that these people have lived with unbearable noise levels for three years rather than confronting the issue. But, of course, they don't want to seem rude. And there is nothing ruder than acknowledging that you don't love being in close quarters with someone else's child.

Again, it's about being the right kind of rude. Picking your moment. Phrasing it nicely. Allowing the parents in question a few weeks to get used to their new circumstances before making a complaint. Sticking to your guns but offering your complaint politely, and with a smile. As is so often (annoyingly) the case, no one is right or wrong in this situation. As such, all you can do is be calm, direct and constructive in your feedback. Having a go at a neighbour who has a baby just because you want to feel heard is the wrong kind of rude. Much as offloading your rage feels brilliant, it's not fair to subject a stranger to it, especially one with a screaming baby and a total lack of sleep. If you need to offload, talk to someone else and be as rage-filled as you want. The right kind of rude would be to speak to the neighbour in an attempt to achieve something, not simply to have a rant. Offering a constructive solution (Have you got carpets? Would you consider better sound-proofing? Could either of us move bedrooms?) is the right kind of rude.

The right kind of rude: to your friends

- Your friends are some of the hardest people to be rude to, especially if you have known them for a long time and set the expectation that you will behave in a certain way. However, good friends will be understanding (if a little surprised) when you announce a regime change.

- It's normal for friendships to ebb and flow, feeling closer to different people at different times. It is not your responsibility (or even possible) to keep every single one of your friendships in perfect harmony at all times.

- Friendships should be about give and take. If you come away from every meeting feeling drained, having only talked about the other person, then that friendship is not working for you.

- When your friends have children, it will change their lives. You are not obliged to change yours unless you want to.

- A little bit of bitching and gossiping is normal – women

have been socialised to talk about each other rather than to each other. That said, if you are constantly expressing the same frustrations about the same person, that's a compass reading for your true feelings about them and you should follow it.

- Sometimes friendships need break-ups, just like relationships do.

- Friendship groups where everyone gets on brilliantly and you're all equally close to each other are fiction. Liberate yourself from that aspiration and you'll feel a whole lot freer.

- You are not an unpaid therapist and if someone is using you as such, you have the right to set boundaries.

- That said, you should expect people to mirror the boundaries you set for them. Being rude doesn't mean being unreasonable, and you can't make the 3 a.m. 'Why doesn't he love me?' call if you've told your girlfriends that you will have friendship office hours between 11 a.m. and 1 p.m. on Tuesdays and Thursdays.

Princess Margaret

Princess Margaret (1930–2002) was the younger sister of Queen Elizabeth II. While being polite is part of Queen Elizabeth's job description, Margaret was bound by no such qualms. She was, without a doubt, a gloriously rude woman.

While the British monarchy is founded on incongruous parsimoniousness (they apparently do a £10 gift limit at Christmas), Margaret had a talent for leaning in to luxury. A diary of her daily routine claimed that she started the morning at 9 a.m. with breakfast in bed, followed by two hours in bed listening to the radio, reading the newspapers ('which she invariably left scattered over the floor') and chain-smoking. The job of a royal is mostly to cut ribbons, shake hands and pretend that you're interested in whoever you're talking to. It's the very antithesis of being rude. And yet Margaret had a skill that so many of us struggle with: saying no.

The princess was once at a party in Chelsea when George Harrison, who had recently been arrested, charged and bailed for possessing drugs, came up to her and told her that he was in trouble. He claimed that the police had 'planted a big block of hash in my bedroom closet'. Margaret expressed her sympathy with the situation, at which point Harrison asked her whether she might be able to get the charges dropped, which she almost certainly could have done. Rather than feeling the need to offer to try, she simply said: 'I don't really think so. It could become a little sticky.'

Since time immemorial princesses are deployed in stories to guide little girls into behaving in a certain way. Cinderella, the most famous princess of all, is rewarded with a pretty dress, some new shoes and a rich husband because she suffers through an abusive childhood without complaint or confrontation. Not exactly a message fit for the modern age. Princess Margaret could not have been further from the simpering sweetness of Cinderella.

The actor Derek Jacobi comes up a cropper, as told in Craig Brown's *Ma'am Darling*:

> There were eight of us and I sat next to her. She smoked continuously, not even putting out her cigarette when the soup arrived, but instead leaning it up against the ashtray. We got on terribly well, very chummy, talking about her mum and her

sister, and she really made me feel like I was a friend, until she got a cigarette out and I picked up a lighter and she snatched it out of my hand and gave it to a ballet dancer called David Wall. 'You don't light my cigarette, dear. Oh no, you're not that close.'

Mean? Absolutely. But again, a skill. How many of us have allowed people to be over-familiar with us in a way which felt uncomfortable and we said nothing, for fear of seeming stuck up? Margaret had no such qualms. When she didn't like something, rather than putting up with it, she made a fuss. Given the number of women I have spoken to when writing this book who were terrified of making a fuss, perhaps it is Princess Margaret we need as a role model, not Cinderella.

CHAPTER TWO

RUDE TO YOUR FAMILY

It is common, as a child, to think that other people's families are better than your own. Your friends from school invariably had a superior type of cereal than you did or were allowed to get their ears pierced much younger than you were. And then, sometime in your twenties, you realise not just that everyone's families are messed up, but that there is a kind of Fibonacci sequence of fucked-upness which enables everyone to have their own special brand of mad.

On top of that there's the issue of respect. Depending on how traditional your family is, there may or may not be a culture of respect in your household – a sense that because your parents raised you, you owe them some deference. I wasn't raised that way. In fact, the area of my life where I am most at ease with rudeness is with my family. I call my parents by their first names, I drink with them, smoke in front of them, talk openly and honestly about my feelings, and as such we're an incredibly close-knit family. They're my favourite people to spend time with, and by choice I would socialise with my siblings and parents (and husband) above any other group.

Rudeness is a big part of why that happened. When I was a teenager and my friends' parents were setting rules left right and centre about how they had to come home, have dinner, spend time as a family, my parents honestly didn't give a fuck. They had a vibrant social life, loads of friends, and no interest in spending time with their children if it was under duress. The only sacrosanct part of the week was Sunday lunch. Just as lots of Jewish families have Friday night dinner, we had Sunday lunch, a time in the week when we all sat round and talked about everything. There's an old saying that you should avoid sex, religion and politics at the table. My family see that more as a to-do list than subjects to be avoided. Despite the fact that my parents are both quite traditional types, Sunday lunch topics over the years have included anal bleaching, sex tapes and how the Kardashian family works (my father can just about name the main siblings, but the children elude him).

As far as I'm concerned, my parents are the perfect rude parents. They had busy lives and they weren't desperate for our approval or our interest. They wanted us to be busy enjoying our friends and exploring the world, and they created a safe, warm place with wine and cake to come back to if and when we needed to. Failure was encouraged, debate was obligatory and anyone who waited for an invitation to speak would find that they were silent for a long time.

The first time my husband visited we had only been dating for a few months. He arrived with a bottle of wine and lots of nice manners, but by the end of dinner on the first night he was shell-shocked. We'd been screaming at each other across the table, debating something (probably Brexit or Love Island), and everyone was drinking, swearing and interrupting each other – just about managing not to throw food, but only just. My sweet husband from his well-mannered, nicely behaved family had arrived expecting a placid evening of polite conversation, and had accidentally stumbled into the rudeness epicentre of the Home Counties.

Of course, however much fun my family are, they still raised me, and I still fail every single day in my quest to be rude. So even great rude parents can turn out children who struggle to say the word 'no'.

When I decided to start introducing the power of rude into my life, the hardest place to do it was with my family – because they are the people who most struggle to see me as a person who can change. It's not their fault and it's not my fault. It's just a fact that the people who raise you, and the people who are raised with you, have a very static attitude towards you. Often our parents put us into boxes as children. It doesn't matter if you've got a modelling contract and your sister has a Nobel Prize; if as children your parents assigned you the clever label and her the pretty one, then that may well be how they regard you for the rest of your life.

In my experience, any active or conscious choice to change yourself creates strife within a family unit. It's born of a good thing – your family love you and therefore don't feel that you need to change yourself. Change is scary, and often looks like a rejection of the past. The past is when you were most connected to your family, so it's entirely understandable that when you announce you want to diverge from it, it doesn't go down well. In my family, it's laughter that is most commonly used as a way of reacting. Brushed off as 'just teasing', having people whom you love laugh at you can be hurtful. If your family are like mine and they're quick to find your attempts at personal development amusing, try to understand that it's almost certainly not supposed to be malicious, it's just their way of finding an outlet for their discomfort.

If you have the kind of parents who think that respect for your elders is extremely important and continue to see you as a child into adulthood, I'll be honest with you: it's worth assessing whether you are up for the fight. If you want to have a genuine and honest relationship with your parents then, yes, you do need to tell them that you are bisexual, that you're vegan, that you're living with your boyfriend out of wedlock or that you're quitting your job to start your own cushion-making business. Every time you take out your nose ring on the way back to their house, lie about having a significant other, pretend you've been promoted or make a reference to your 'savings account', you are making a heavy choice. But, just as I concluded in the dating chapter – that it's OK to do or say whatever you need to do in order to keep yourself safe – it's also entirely reasonable to evaluate what you will get out of radical rudeness towards your family.

You are not a failure if the power of rude needs to stop at your parents' front door. Lots of people are different in every aspect of their lives other than at home. Some parents will never understand their children's life choices, and if you try to force them to get it you are only going to make yourself more unhappy. News management is not a failure. Presenting your parents with what they want to see and then going home to live your authentic life is not wrong. Perhaps it's a kind of positive rudeness in itself.

Regression

One of the things I least like about myself is that when I go home to my family, especially at Christmas, I become a teenager again. I know I'm not alone, but every single December I resolve that I will not let it happen, and yet by Christmas Eve I am physically fighting with my sister for the remote control and throwing a strop because I don't think that my brother is pulling his weight with the washing-up. Experts have suggested that we owe this regression to the fact that we are retracing the old steps we once walked before, putting ourselves physically back in time and therefore following suit emotionally. There's no doubt that that is true. But I think it's also about lingering feelings and thoughts which you haven't expressed.

Your parents will have hurt you, there's no question about that. However great they are, there will have been times when they fucked things up and made you unhappy. If you've got a decent adult relationship, then you probably don't want to bring up those things. Why drag it all out again? Why look for an argument? Why be rude? But if you don't risk upsetting your parents and lancing those boils, they just get (to continue a really gross metaphor) bigger, angrier and more painful. When you go home and steep yourself in the memories of the hurt you experienced as a young person, but don't allow yourself any outlet for them, you force yourself back into that impotent, childlike state in which your emotions were written off as 'being hormonal' and you didn't get much of a vote because you were 'one of the kids'. Suddenly you're back in your bedroom, slamming doors and playing loud music because they're the only small ways in which you can have control over your environment.

When I was a teenager, my parents were very concerned about my weight, which seems odd because I wasn't an especially heavy child. Not skinny, but just sort of normal. Anyway, they were worried about it and tried all sorts of things: getting me a personal trainer, obligatory exercise before being allowed to watch TV, offering me a whole new wardrobe if I lost weight. It's a common concept, bribing your children to lose weight. Many of my female friends who were slightly heavier as teens were offered money or even cars if they shed the pounds.

Unsurprisingly, this only served to make me completely, absolutely, utterly obsessed with my weight. It will, without question, be the thing which I expend most energy thinking about at the end of my life. And I am very angry about that. I was born without any of this, and thanks to my parents' interest, bordering on obsession, with my weight, I experimented with bulimia and I've been either on a diet, or bingeing because I've fallen off a diet, since I was eleven.

I don't talk to them about this. I don't want to. Ironic, given that I've written about it in a book, but I suppose I'm hoping that they won't read it; because despite the fact that they are incredible, wonderful, brilliant people who love me beyond all possibility, I am still furious about their behaviour concerning my weight. But I don't want to kick that wasps' nest. I don't want to talk about it. I don't want to throw all the glorious things about my idyllic childhood back at them because they looked ashen-faced when I wanted to eat a Magnum. But there is a price to pay for my refusal to be 'rude' to them about their attitude to my weight. When I am around them, food, weight, body image – it's all a tinderbox. I definitely can't enjoy pigging out on anything and everything I want to eat on festive family occasions (unless I've been dieting and look/feel thinner than usual).

It might not be your weight. It might be your sexuality, your career, your dating history – the list of possibilities is half a mile long – but there is probably an area of your life which you don't want to discuss with your parents. And if you're like me and you really can't, that's OK. But if you *can* find a way to be 'rude' to your parents, in the sense that you're willing to suspend the happy fiction many of us engage in as adults, so that all the scars of childhood heal, then you might well be able to tackle the root cause of your anger. But if you don't manage it, then please know that you are far from alone, and I'm right there with you, secretly sobbing over not getting the last green Quality Street triangle.

Siblings

Siblings can be both the greatest blessing and the biggest pain in the arse – all of the love you feel for your closest friends, topped with a sense of obligation that only a shared childhood or bloodline can create. Many of us find that the easiest people in the world to be rude to are our siblings, probably because we grew up stealing their toys and then their clothes, screaming, 'I hate you' at them and often coming to physical blows. In many ways we should try to model our friendships on our sibling relationships, because they are not hindered by the kind of politeness we seem to exercise towards people we're friends with. However, the flip side of that entrenched comfortability with your siblings is that it becomes very easy for them to take the piss, and it can feel really difficult to tell them to stop.

My beloved younger brother, now an upstanding citizen and exemplary human being, drove me up the wall when he spent a whole summer staying at my flat rent-free while he was working at a department store in central London. While, initially, it was lovely to have him there, I soon found myself tidying up the plates and cups left in his bedroom, and then one day I found a bag of Indian take-away tied up under the bed with one of my plates and knives and forks inside it. I felt like his mum. But I complained about it without actually doing anything to change the situation, because I love him, and he's my brother.

Petra, twenty-four, says:

My brother asks for money a lot. He's at uni, I know he's quite broke, and my parents won't give it to him. He thinks I'm really well off because I have a job, and I don't earn badly, but I've got to pay rent, buy food, all that stuff. By the time I've given him a hundred quid it means that I can't do things that I want to do. But he's my baby brother. I don't think I can tell him no. I tried to talk to him about paying me back and he keeps making noises about doing it when he graduates, but that's still a long while off. I've given him twelve hundred quid over the last two years. When I worked out how much it was, I actually felt a bit sick. I resent it – it's my money! But I love him so much and I hate the idea of him staying in while his friends go out because he hasn't got any money.

Partners

A few months after I started going out with my husband, I was in the bath at his house and I accidentally sort of flooded the floor. Nothing major, I just overfilled the tub and then got in, spilling hot water all over the tiles. I was mortified. Genuinely mortified. I apologised fifteen, twenty times, acting like I'd killed his best unicorn. Six months later I accidentally shrank his jumper in the washing machine – a jumper that I happened to hate. I laughed so hard at the teeny-tiny garment and his outrage at its loss that I thought I might rupture something. My point here is that somewhere between the bath and the jumper, I stopped being polite to him.

We talk a lot about the honeymoon period in a relationship being over, and yes, that is hard. When the very idea of seeing your boyfriend naked ceases to send you into a tailspin, and you don't always get out of bed to brush your teeth before pretending to have just woken up minty-fresh, things are changing. But that's also around the time when you lose the fear of being rude to them.

You cannot build a life with a person whom you're afraid to

be rude to. The key is to make it the kind of rudeness which brings you closer. When our honeymoon period drew to an end, I held an amnesty with my husband (boyfriend at the time), a chance to tell all the uncomfortable truths that we needed to air in order to move forward. 'I didn't actually do an Economics A-Level,' I started, citing a lie I'd told during a debate in our early days to add weight during an argument. 'I don't like falling asleep cuddling,' I told him, because after six months of a cricked neck and twisted spine it was time to put sleep quality above cuteness. 'And I think that pub in Waterloo that you love is one of the worst places I've ever been drinking in my life.'

I said it nicely, and I mentioned lots of things that I loved about him too. Then I asked him to do the same. He was tentative, sensing that this might be some kind of a trap, but eventually he told me that he thought I made a shit cup of tea (true), that he didn't want to listen to Taylor Swift every single day (we're still fighting on that one) and that sometimes when I make jokes at his expense it hurts his feelings.

Rudeness – that is to say, being candid about things which other couples might let go – is the bedrock on which we built our marriage. And although our marriage is a long way from perfect, it helped.

These days we have a marriage MOT every couple of months. We wait until we're in a really good mood with each other and feeling fully loved up, then we go out to dinner, drink a bottle of wine and talk about what's working, what's not working, what we want to change and what we want to do more of. My husband hasn't always found this easy – he's one of life's repressors – but he would tell you (or at least he tells me) that it's a central part of what makes us work as a couple.

In-laws

The only parents more difficult to deal with than your own are your in-laws. I'm fortunate because my husband's parents are enormously tolerant of me, despite the fact that I regularly go on television to talk about my sex life, but when I first met them I was terrified. I've never been keener to repress my rude and ballsy personality than I was on my initial visit to stay with them. Of course, as is so often the case, in doing so I made myself seem quite strange. I was so busy trying to come across as perfect that I stopped concentrating on anything other than being polite, which was how I ended up leaving a pair of my knickers in my husband's childhood bed and eschewing every single one of my political and social opinions, lest I give offence. It's so often the case with the fear of being rude that you can become so obsessed with getting it 'right' that you end up getting it completely wrong.

While I've been lucky with my in-laws, that's not the case for everyone. And when you're saddled with the combination of bad in-laws and a desire not to offend or upset them, you have a powder keg. Darhla is twenty-six. She recently had a six-month-long relationship with a man named Oliver. A few months in, he took her back to his family home, a sizeable demi-mansion in the Home Counties. 'It was all fine,' she tells me, 'until his mum asked me what form of contraception I was using. She gave me this look when she asked, like refusing to answer would be unacceptable, and when I laughed it off she seemed to think I had admitted that I was trying to baby-trap her son. Then, after dinner, while we were having coffee and liqueurs, she brought out a bag of cocaine and offered everyone a line. I ended up doing one to be polite, as if it was a second helping of lasagne.'

Admittedly, Darhla's experience is pretty extreme – most of our mothers-in-law don't casually offer out class-A drugs as a chaser to a lovely tiramisu – but testing of boundaries and dick-swinging contests are very common. In-laws who want to make your life difficult realise that you're terrified of offending them. Of all the places in the world where you're least likely to want to enjoy the power of rude, it's during a visit to your in-laws; but, however counter-intuitive it might sound, I think that's why it's so important to pull out the rude straight away.

Rose, twenty-eight, has been going out with her boyfriend Matt for seven years:

> We go on holiday with his parents every year, because he's an only child and they're a very close-knit family. I knew that when I got involved. He's never going to stop going on the holiday with them, so either he goes on his own or I come along. In theory, it would be fine, but his father seems to get a real kick out of winding me up. I work in wine, so whenever we're drinking a bottle he'll hide the label and get me to guess what grape it is. If I'm wrong, he absolutely loves it.
>
> Plus, he talks to me like I'm a little Victorian orphan, saying things like, 'I know it's a big villa that we're renting, don't worry it wasn't that expensive, you don't need to chip in,' even though I've offered to and they won't let me. My boyfriend chooses not to see it, he says it's his dad being playful, so I nod and smile and think about the super-budget old people's home I'm going to put him in one day.

Refusing to be rude to your in-laws where necessary is a false economy. We as humans like and respect strong people. Weakness is not an attractive quality, unless you're the sort of person who enjoys manipulating and controlling others. So when you resist your boyfriend's mum's offer of another super-strength gin and tonic, you're not being rude, you're demonstrating that you're your own woman. Your in-laws will not like you more if you waver in your vegetarianism because they forgot and cooked sausages.

There is a popular phrase on Mumsnet (the source of so much wisdom): 'You don't have an in-law problem, you have a husband problem.' The consensus is that if your other half is willing to watch his parents being rude to you, he's the real issue, not them. And I agree – the most important thing about rudeness and in-laws is to make sure that your partner is on the same page as you. If you go back to his childhood bedroom after supper and he starts bollocking you for debating with his mother, or saying no to his father's suggestion of another helping of mashed potatoes, then honestly run. Don't get involved with someone who automatically sides with their parents over you – that way lies ruin.

Extended family

Every year, as the leaves turn golden and the air grows cold, people all over the world gird their loins as they prepare to return home and survive the barrage of offensive, inappropriate and frustrating questions from their family. The Thanksgiving or Christmas dinner table is one of the only places in the world where you can watch a gender-queer vegan sit next to a Nigel Farage superfan boomer. There should be something nice about the idea of everyone reaching across political lines to celebrate the holidays together, but, in reality, it just seems to bring out the worst in all of us. Those who tend towards the old school and right-wing politics become desperate to prove that they're not compromising their values so as not to 'trigger a snowflake', and those of us who are lefty liberals find ourselves getting wound up so tightly we could snap at any point, driven mad by comments which should probably be ignored.

Embracing the power of rude does not mean getting into a fight every single time someone tries to start one. In fact, it is the opposite. The power of rude is about not giving people what they want, unless you want to give it, or see a good reason to do so. When a member of your extended family tries to start a 'debate' about immigration or feminism, or pretty much anything, the rudest possible thing you can do is refuse to rise to it, smile and say, 'I'm not sure this is for the table, Uncle Simon. More peas?'

Trying to 'educate' the people around you about why their trash opinions are trash is all very noble, but you are never going to change someone's mind if they aren't open to listening to you. Instead, all you'll do is add to the perception that you're an intolerant snowflake or an emotional brat. If anyone at the dinner is actually open to hearing what you have to say, then knock yourself out with the conversion lecture, throw facts about immigration or Brexit their way, but at least make an assessment before you give emotional effort to this conversation. Is it really worth it? Or are you going to be pushed into being the wrong kind of rude and end up adding fuel to their 'millennials are pathetic babies' fire?

It is not easy to sit at a table with someone whose views you find abhorrent, but there is no point in wasting your time and energy trying to change that with debate. If you do want to try to convince anyone of anything, asserting yourself as a calm, reasoned and rational person is an essential first step. Perhaps not fair, but entirely true.

You are also entirely within your rights to be rude in the sense of disengaging. If you can stand up, smile and walk away, then do. If not, then turn and speak to someone else at the table or change the topic of conversation. You do not owe anyone a conversation about anything, even during dinner. You don't have to sugar-coat your distaste for the conversation or rely on the old 'no religion or politics at the table' line; you can be far more honest than that. Saying, 'I don't feel like talking about this' or 'I'm not sure either of us are going to benefit from this conversation' makes your point quickly and squarely, with a nice undertone of 'I'm the real adult here.'

Motherhood

I think of my mother as pretty much the perfect parent. She made mistakes, obviously, because she is human, but, while there were times when we screamed at each other and weeks when I considered her to be my mortal enemy, I've now reached my late twenties and see my mum as one of my closest friends, and look back on my childhood as generally really happy.

My mother, however, seems to feel differently. She carries enormous guilt about the fact that she worked when we were children, that she had childcare and that she wasn't willing to suspend her every wish the moment I arrived in the world, until her youngest baby was twenty-one years old. The things that I most admire about her – her career, her social network, the fullness of the life that she lived around having children – are the things that she feels worst about. While I view her as the archetypal rude parent, I'm quite sure she would tell you that she felt she was messing the whole thing up, pretty much the entire time.

I'm not a parent, and so it would be wrong for me to attempt to give any advice about being one; but what I have observed as an outsider is that, unlike many other things in life, parenting seems to have the ability to make you feel wrong when you are doing it completely right. You might know on paper that leaving your child with a babysitter or at nursery is right, but their screaming makes it feel wrong. You might be totally convinced that spending time on your own or with your friends is an essential part of retaining your sanity, but again, when you're out in a pub sneaking off to the loo to look at pictures of your baby on your phone, it feels wrong, as if you're going against the grain of motherhood.

When you become a mother, you suddenly have to advocate both for yourself and for your child. The world seems temporarily to become your enemy: a place full of physical and emotional barriers, be it the flights of stairs with no lifts for your buggy, or the fact that strangers will happily comment on your choice to bottle- or breast-feed, your baby's napping schedule – in short almost everything you do. And your options at this point are to drown in your own guilt, or to embrace the power of rude. The majority of the women who took the *Rude* survey said that they felt braver and more confident after they had children.

Clara is thirty-five and has one daughter. She told me a story which seemed to exemplify the change that motherhood can inspire:

> I was in a café with my daughter when she was a few months old. She'd barely slept the night before, but was finally chilling out in the pram, sleepy and not making a fuss. I was playing on my phone, looking at everyone else's weekends and feeling jealous of everyone who'd gone out to the pub and not needed to put nipple towels in their bra to soak up breast milk. A woman at the next table remarked to her husband that it's 'so sad how you only ever see mothers on their phones these days' and I lost my mind.

I am not a confrontational person; I hate a fight. But I couldn't let it go. I interrupted and told her that I'd been alone with the baby for four days because my husband was travelling and that this was the first moment I'd had to myself, that it was none of her business and to leave me alone. She was horrified, and then apologetic. Then they left. And I felt triumphant because I'd always been the person who came up with the perfect retort four hours later or bit my tongue because I didn't want to have an argument, but here I was shouting at this total stranger for mum-shaming me.

My big question about this story was how Clara felt afterwards. Did she regret losing her temper and giving way to her anger? Apparently not. 'I shouldn't have shouted,' she says. 'I should have said it calmly, but I was glad I said something and honestly if the options were to lose my temper or say nothing, I'm glad I lost my temper. She needed to know that you can't try to make people feel bad about their parenting for fun.'

While Clara might have been on the slightly more aggressive side of what the power of rude endorses, it's certainly true that the feeling of wishing you had said something to a person who has hurt you is corrosive, and sometimes you do need to respond full-force. As long as that full force isn't physical or abusive, there's no point in feeling guilty afterwards.

Doing better

Given that our phobia of being rude was most likely instilled in us by our parents (they fuck you up, and all that), it follows that we have a choice as to whether or not to hand that phobia on to our kids, something of which many of the parents I've spoken to are aware and are actively trying to combat in the next generation.

The most common theme I have heard from people who currently have young children is that they will no longer make their children hug or kiss family members and friends if they don't want to. Sophie, who has two daughters, says:

> I was always forced to kiss all of my parents' friends and family goodbye when we left a party. To this day, I'll try to leave a party without saying goodbye to everyone, on the basis that I hate it. When my daughter was younger, I read an article about how you shouldn't make your kids kiss or hug anyone they don't want to, so that you teach them to have autonomy over their bodies. It's an easy way to teach them about consent from a really early age. When I read it something just clicked, but I also felt really angry – like I'd been let down by my own childhood. My parents prioritised the feelings of other adults above mine. They taught me, admittedly without meaning to, that it was rude to withhold physical affection from people who made me uncomfortable, a lesson that I continued to believe for much of my life.
>
> With my daughters, I ask them to say goodbye nicely, or to wave. Some of our family members have been offended when they've asked for a hug and been told no, but because I'm doing it for my daughters, I've got this total lack of fear about being rude. I still hug or kiss people when I arrive at a party, even though I hate doing it, because I can't be rude for myself, but I can do it on behalf of my kids, and I like to think that the people-pleasing will end with me.

The ability to be rude on behalf of your children when you've always struggled to do it for yourself is a common theme, as if it's more viable to suspend the rules ingrained in you if it is to protect your child rather than to take care of yourself.

It's beyond encouraging to see that so many parents are teaching their children that their own bodily autonomy is important. By not forcing your children to hug or kiss strangers, you are conveying the message that their comfort with physical contact is more important than the potential to give offence by refusing it. The earlier we can teach young people this, the less likely they are to tolerate unwanted physical attention in adulthood.

The right kind of rude: to your family

- You do not owe your family a free pass to do or say as they please towards you, just because you are related. Yes, family is important, but anyone who makes you feel badly about yourself or your life is fair game for the rude treatment.

- Some people are not close to their families. That is OK. You have not failed because you don't get on with your siblings or because your mum is not your best friend. Sometimes family is the people you choose.

- Other people's families are deep, dark magic and incredibly difficult to navigate – it's OK if you never really nail it with your in-laws.

- However, your partner should be on your side, or at least try to play an active role in smoothing any friction between you and his family.

- Starting your own family (or rather, continuing it – two people can of course be a family on their own) is a scary business, but it does give you a chance to assess what in your own childhood was not ideal, and to think about how you want to counter it.

- It's easy to take a very polemic attitude towards your childhood: either it was happy, or it was unhappy. But, in reality, it was most likely a mixture of both. Needing to talk to your parents about the unhappy aspects of your childhood does not mean that you are ungrateful.

Meghan Markle, aka the Duchess of Sussex

Meghan Markle was born in 1981, in Los Angeles. Then, thirty-five years later, she met a prince, fell in love and the entire world lost their fucking minds.

The 'Demanding Duchess', 'Birth Brat', 'Princess Pushy' – the insulting nicknames came thick and fast, sometimes even from members of her own family. For the high crime of not wanting to erase her entire personality and set of values (she's a proud feminist), Meghan has been crucified in the press over and over again. If she sneezes, she's spreading germs to innocent people. If she uses a tissue, she doesn't care about the mass-slaughter of trees. I'm exaggerating here, but only a little bit.

Meghan is a kindred spirit in the sense that she is not naturally rude. When she first started to take part in royal life, she did pretty much everything she could possibly have done to make the British public and the Royal Family like her. Remember when she went to a family function a few days after her wedding wearing the world's most horrific 'nude' tights? Remember how she went on a day-long train journey with her husband's grandmother? And smiled at children day after day after day? Then, like me, and hopefully like you, she had had enough. She realised that smiling and waving and being sweet wasn't going to get her what she wanted (and what she wanted was basically to marry the man she loved, help out in the family business and get on with it). She embraced the power of rude.

It started small. Well, as small as putting a load of incredible high-profile super-woke women on the cover of *Vogue* can possibly be. Then she and Harry started to make decisions based on what they wanted – breaking away and forming their own charity, redoing their home, filming a charity video with Ed Sheeran (we don't forgive you for that last one, but we all make mistakes). Predictably, the press went mad about this. They were punished for decorating their house when the details of their refurb ended up online, sandwiched next to the words 'taxpayers' money', as if the entire royal deal isn't taxpayers' money. The *Vogue* cover was smacked down with public critique of their use of a private jet. Their choice not to make the birth of their son a fully public event resulted in opinion pieces about how they 'owe' us photos of their child, and some catty side-eye about Meghan's 'post-birth body'.

Lots of people would have curled back into their shell, chastised by media attempts to shut them up, and abandoned the gospel of rude. But not Meghan. Instead, she and Harry took the unprecedented step of instructing a lawyer – their own lawyer, not the Royal Family's default firm – and announcing that Meghan – specifically Meghan – was suing the *Mail on Sunday* for reproducing a letter sent by her father, Thomas Markle, without her consent.

In his statement explaining what he and Meghan had decided to do, Harry wrote: 'Though this action may not be the safe one, it is the right one. Because my deepest fear is history repeating itself. I've seen what happens when someone I love is commoditised to the point that they are no longer treated or seen as a real person. I lost my mother and now I watch my wife falling victim to the same powerful forces.'

The lawsuit wasn't where the story ended, though. A few

weeks later the couple embarked on a press tour of South Africa, accompanied by the journalist Tom Bradby. During the course of the documentary, he asked Meghan about her experience of joining the Royal Family. She answered candidly, prioritising telling the truth above sparing anyone else's feelings in a way that had me punching the air. 'Thank you for asking if I'm OK,' she told the camera. 'Not many people have.' It was in that moment that Meghan became my power of rude icon.

Social media, the press, the entire bloody country went into overdrive: 'ungrateful', 'spoiled', 'entitled'. Commentators asked how a woman with so much money could possibly dare to say that she was having a hard time, to reject the hospitality of the British Royal Family. And while it's true that the backdrop of South Africa, a country with its fair share of issues, was perhaps not the perfect optics for a conversation about struggle, the point is that Meghan broke the number-one rule of being a royal: she spoke freely and openly about her feelings, not with a polished statement written by a group of professionals, but in her own voice. It was bold, brave, brilliant and rude.

The next day I was in the lift at work and a woman in front of me was WhatsApping her friends. 'Did you see it?' she wrote. 'Yes, I fucking hate her,' replied the friend. 'Me too,' said the woman in front of me. 'She's an ungrateful bitch. And I'm so sick of those shirt dresses.'

I was shocked that Meghan's radical honesty could have elicited such blind rage in complete strangers. But I suppose that's the depressing reality of being rude: there are people who are going to decide to be angry about it, without giving any consideration to why they feel that way. Their frustrations will abound without any justification or examination, and you just have to live with that.

*

Meghan is a perfect example of the fact that being a rude woman doesn't mean being charmless or bad-mannered. You can still be sweet, loving, generous and polite, but on your own terms.

NB: At the time of writing, Harry and Meghan have just handed in their notice to the Royal Family – the ultimate, air-punching act of well-executed rudeness.

CHAPTER THREE

RUDE DATING

Full disclosure: it's been a little while since I was on the dating scene. I met my husband (at time of writing) aged twenty-two, got engaged at twenty-four and married at twenty-six. When I announced that I was getting hitched, various people asked me if I thought I was going to miss out on things, committing myself to a relationship so young – which seems an odd thing to ask a newly engaged woman, but that's by the by. The answer was a solid and reverberating no. I was not sad about it, because I didn't want to date. Dating, in my experience, is an absolute hellscape, and the five years that I'd spent having sex, relationships and everything in between had been messy, painful and complicated. Made worse by the fact that I, like many women, was blighted by an inability to offend.

When I used to go clubbing as a teenager my friends and I would dance in a circle. Men would come up behind us, grab our hips and start dancing behind us, which pretty much just meant rubbing their crotch against your arse/back depending on how tall you were. Often that entailed having a stranger's semi-erect penis gyrating against the small of your naked back (it was the noughties; low-waisted jeans were the thing). Rather than pulling away or even asking security to remove the penis-rubber, my friends and I would just rotate the circle until we reached a different part of the dance floor in safety. We never remonstrated with the man, or made any kind of formal complaint. We just brushed it off. Because, as you'll notice is rather a theme here, we didn't want to be rude. We assumed that because we were dressed up and dancing, these men had a right to attempt to fuck us, and that it was our responsibility to let them down gently.

Dating is now more commonly about apps than clubs, but the central point remains the same. Politeness is apparently the price that women are obliged to pay for attempting to navigate the world of dating.

Rude to be kind

When I was in my early twenties, I dated a very sweet guy who had a super-well-paid job in the Middle East. He was a tax exile and only allowed to spend ninety days a year in the UK, so to see each other we had to meet in European cities. I was twenty-one, smitten and initially very into this arrangement. As a broke student, the whole thing was desperately exciting. To start with it worked well: we spent a happy week travelling around Paris and the South of France, and I couldn't quite believe my luck. But a couple of months later I went back to university, got tangled up in my life as a twenty-year-old student and realised that an international relationship wasn't going to work for me any more.

What I should have done was tell him straight that I'd had a brilliant time, but that I wanted us to stop seeing each other. But, having spent my whole life trying not to offend people who had been mean to me, I had no idea how I was supposed to do this to someone who had been beyond generous and kind. I was due to visit him in Italy, and as the date of my flight grew closer I got more and more panicked. The day before the flight I came down with a violent cold and developed an abscess on my gum, meaning that I could hardly eat anything, but still I packed my bags, flew to Italy and desperately tried to put on a brave face.

Upon arrival I practically passed out and spent the afternoon watching *Harry Potter* in the fancy hotel bed. I couldn't eat anything at the nice restaurants, I could barely bring myself to finish a cocktail. I was horrible company and completely miserable. We would both have been happier if I had stayed at home in bed, but of course he was being so generous and kind, and I was so terrified of being ungrateful, that I'd ended up giving us both a miserable weekend.

We broke up on the Sunday morning after a calm and resigned conversation at breakfast. I took a bus back to the airport because I didn't want to inconvenience him by sticking around his hotel room, arrived six hours too early for my flight and slept off the flu on an airport floor. If I'd had the confidence to say no to the trip I'd have saved myself a lot of time and aggro, but I'd also have saved him some. My desire not to be rude made me the absolute worst version of myself.

Sometimes, as in the example above, a fear of being rude might start off being about protecting someone else's feelings but end up being about protecting your own. While the idea of wanting to avoid causing any hurt is noble and nice, it can be counterproductive and hurtful to everyone involved. It's impossible to have a meaningful relationship with someone if you are afraid to hurt their feelings or be rude to them.

If I told you that someone was 'scared of being rude', you would probably automatically assume that this meant that they were nice. But that's the thing: my fear of being rude didn't make me nice. It made me conflict-averse, which in turn made me into a coward. I avoided telling people uncomfortable truths which really needed to be spoken about, and I allowed myself to believe that it was out of deference to their feelings, when really it was about my own. Yes, some of my rude-phobia was about having been socialised as a woman and a societal expectation to behave in a specific way, but there was also an element of my desire to be liked, wanted and even loved.

That feeling – that you want to be loved – is even worse when you're dating. In the early days, there's huge pressure to represent yourself as the best of the best. Generally speaking, this means that men and women dial up the values they are traditionally expected to exemplify: men being bold and brash and outgoing; women being sweet and kind and supportive, which (yes, you know what's coming) is the opposite of rude.

Tinder, Bumble, Hinge and God knows what comes next

When I met my husband and hung up my dating hat, Tinder was still a new-ish phenomenon which came with a healthy side of stigma – a raised eyebrow and a snarky comment about how 'Rachel met her boyfriend on *Tinder*', the subtext being that Rachel had to go crawling for Internet boyfriends on a sex website. Half a decade on, meeting people on apps is pretty much the default. In lots of ways it's a miracle. It means that you can link up with people who are outside your social circle, has reduced the popularity of dating in the workplace, which often made life very awkward, and enables people with specific or niche interests to connect with each other. But there's also no denying that operating from behind a screen has changed things. Dating apps have blurred the boundaries of acceptable behaviour.

Men in real life rarely expose themselves to women, yet unsolicited dick pics are a way of life for the modern dater. Similarly, online dating has given rise to a whole host of nasty behaviours with catchy names, including but not limited to: catfishing, ghosting, zombieing, submarining, breadcrumbing and benching. All of which stem from a fear of being the good kind of rude – which means behaving in the bad kind of rude way.

An easy example: I once went on a date with a man who had chronic asthma, thought that arts funding should be cut and didn't like swearing. I was at the time a committed smoker and aspiring playwright whose favourite word was 'fuck'. After we clawed our way through a ninety-minute drink, we went in opposite directions in both a literal and a metaphorical sense. There was no question that we would ever see each other again and yet, to his credit, he sent me a text saying he didn't think the chemistry was there but that he enjoyed the bar I had chosen. Job done. As it happens, I was not on the edge of my seat, hoping that he would message me, but if I had been I'd have read the message, been briefly deflated and then moved on with my life.

On the flipside, on another occasion I went for a drink with a man called Rupert I met through a temping job on whom I had a massive crush. Everything about him did it for me. We went for a drink and I hung on his every word, and then we entered into a protracted back-and-forth messaging situation whereby he would suggest meeting up and then cancel, again and again and again. Eventually he demi-ghosted me. During this period, whenever I met someone who might be a sensible romantic prospect, I wrote them off instantly because as soon as Rupert changed his mind and realised I was the perfect woman, we were going to fall in love and get married.

I have no doubt that Rupert would tell you that he was letting me down gently, but what he was actually doing was being the wrong kind of rude. Good rude is direct, fair and tactful. Bad rude is self-serving and selfish.

Rejection

No one likes being rejected: it makes you feel bad about yourself, it's uncomfortable and upsetting. And doing the rejecting isn't much fun either, which is possibly why so many women struggle with hurting people's feelings in a romantic context.

The official rude party line is that women should be free and able to reject men whenever they need to, without being hurtful or unkind, but also without resorting to dishonesty. However, that's the kind of thinking which works really well in a theory but not so well in real life.

Sorry, I have a boyfriend

I'm not sure when, as a woman, you learn to say, 'Sorry, I've got a boyfriend' to men in clubs and bars, but it's early on. I remember standing at the bar at a club in West London, freshly eighteen and waiting to buy one of my first legal drinks. An older guy in a suit started chatting me up, and, when I went to return to my friends, tried to come with me. It didn't occur to me to tell him that I wasn't interested or that I wanted to spend the evening with my friends. I, like so many women, reached for the automatic get-out-of-jail-free card: 'I have a boyfriend.' The problem there is that you're effectively using belonging to someone else as a justification for being left alone, when in reality you don't owe any explanation at all.

Yet again, this is an example of women putting their own wants and needs second and someone else's first. OK, it might not kill you to go on a few dates with a person you don't really fancy, or to allow a man to hit on you in a bar to bolster his self-esteem, but why should you? What is the point of allowing this to happen? Why are we so bad at putting ourselves first?

This formula is designed to allow a man to think that, were you not in a committed relationship with someone else, you would be available for him. It is a trope that women of all ages all over the world trot out, and it has one single purpose: to reject a man without him realising that he has been rejected, therefore insulating him from any negative emotions. You could argue that it's a victimless crime. You get left alone and he's allowed to enjoy his evening without feeling rejected, but I'm afraid there is more to it than that. There is a knock-on effect which comes from protecting men from rejection and refusing to be rude to them. People who don't experience rejection don't learn to work with it. It contributes to a culture of entitlement, which in turn creates a bigger problem of harassment.

In 2019, eighteen-year-old Gabrielle Walsh was punched in the face so hard that it knocked her unconscious when she told a man outside a Manchester nightclub that she wasn't interested in him. She didn't opt for the feeling, sparing lie; she told the (very reasonable) truth and, in punishment, the near-stranger smacked her in the face.

Discussing the incident in the *Manchester Evening News*, Gabrielle said:

I'd taken my shoes off and this guy came over and said, 'I like your feet.' I just said OK and tried to walk away. They [her assailant was with a friend] kept walking behind trying to talk to me. Eventually, I turned around and said, 'I'm sorry, I'm not interested.' They kept harassing us, then he hit me – he fully knocked me out.

I'm not a rude person, I just said, 'Sorry, I'm not interested.' I think it was a jealousy, ego thing because I rejected him in front of his friends. Girls feel like they can't say 'no'. They feel like if they say 'no' then [men] might hurt you, and in this case it was true.

There's a joke that goes: 'A girl with a boyfriend, a vegan and someone who went on a gap year walk into a room. Who tells you first?' On the veganism and the gap year, they might have a point. But there's a good reason that women wheel out the words 'I have a boyfriend' early in the conversation: it's to protect ourselves. We don't say, 'I have a boyfriend' because we're pleased with ourselves, or for fun. We do it for our safety. Men seem to respect the fact that we are someone else's property, even when they don't respect our right to say yes or no.

Gabrielle Walsh's experience is not an isolated one. YouTuber Bianca Devins was allegedly murdered by a man whom she rejected romantically. In 2014, Elliot Rodger committed a mass-murder near the campus of University of California in Santa Barbara, citing romantic rejection by multiple women as his reason.

One of the first victims of the Santa Fe school shooting in 2018 was a young woman who had turned the shooter down. The list of cases in which a woman has refused a man and then paid for it with her life goes on and on.

Gabrielle Walsh did the 'right' thing when she told a man she didn't fancy that she wasn't interested. She did the 'rude' thing – the thing that on paper I would cheer her on for, but sometimes doing the right thing has horrible consequences.

In a perfect world, all women would stop sugar-coating rejections. There is no reason why we should feel obliged to say that we have a boyfriend, we're too tired, we're gay or on our way home to see our over-protective spouse instead of telling the truth, but sometimes we have to be pragmatic. Sometimes we have to do the wrong thing for the right reason. Putting a fake diamond on your left ring finger on a night out to avoid giving men the brush-off is pandering, but then sometimes pandering is the safest thing to do.

Of course, there are consequences if women don't say no to men. If a man only ever hears, 'I'm sorry, I have a boyfriend,' then the first time a woman says, 'I'm not interested' it's going to come as a shock. If we can create a culture in which men don't get used to having their romantic feelings protected above all else, then we skip this problem entirely. It's possible that we could raise an entire generation of men who are comfortable with being rejected because a woman isn't attracted to them, not because she's already been claimed by another man.

Being a woman is often like standing on a balance board, trying to spin plates with both hands and keeping a book steady on your head. This is one of those situations. If you never reject men straight out, you contribute to their culture of entitlement. If you do reject them straight out, you risk being the victim of aggression. In the end, all that any of us can do is to be rude when it is safe to do so, while doing whatever we must to protect ourselves.

On a macro level, much of this Catch-22 situation could be prevented if we addressed it in childhood. One of the most unhelpful things we do is to teach children that if a boy likes a girl, he will be aggressive or unkind to her. It is a sort of pseudo truth, widely accepted, that when a boy likes you, he will pull your hair and push you over.

In 2015, a mother posted on Facebook a picture of her four-year-old daughter, who had been hit so hard by a boy at school that she required stitches, with the following statement:

'I bet he likes you.'

Dear man at the registration desk at the children's hospital, I'm positive that you didn't think that statement through. As soon as I heard it, I knew that is where it begins. That statement is where the idea that hurting is flirting begins to set a tone for what is acceptable behaviour. My four-year-old knows, 'That's not how we show we like someone.' That was not a good choice.

In that moment, hurt and in a new place, worried about perhaps getting a shot or stitches, you were a person we needed to help us, and your words of comfort conveyed a message that someone who likes you might hurt you. No. I will not allow that message to be OK. I will not allow it to be louder than: 'That's not how we show we like each other.'

At that desk, you are in a position of influence, whether you realise it or not. You thought you were making the moment lighter. It is time to take responsibility for the messages we as a society give our children. Do not tell my four-year-old who needs stitches from a boy at school hitting her, 'I bet he likes you.'

Can we really be surprised that men lash out against women who reject them if, during childhood, they are taught that being unkind to women they fancy is a normal way to express their feelings? The depressing thing is that much of this damage is already done. We *can* raise our sons to be better than that, and we *will* do so. In turn, their children will grow up in a world where toxic masculinity no longer exists; but we're not dealing with the future, we're dealing with the now, which means navigating a dating scene filled with men who were, as Philip Larkin would have put it, fucked up by their own parents several decades ago. As such we've got no idea where the fault lines might be. Are you rejecting a guy who might go on to be your long-term friend? Or are you rejecting the rare but real man who will take your lack of interest as a reason to do you physical harm, release your nudes on the Internet or follow you around?

Danger

When I was twenty-two, I went to a very expensive London hotel with a man. He was an attractive Canadian, here for work. We had drinks at the bar and he seemed different from his online personality. He implied he was disappointed with my looks, but bought me a second cocktail and kept talking. The understanding had been that I was going to go upstairs with him. So, despite the fact that my spidey senses were screaming, I did. When we got upstairs, I asked him if I could use the bathroom and he said no. I was confused, and something started to seem off. He became edgy and panicked.

I asked him if I could go back downstairs and use the bathroom there and he got frustrated with me. Something was not right. When I tell this story people often suggest that he'd left the bathroom in a mess, but he knew I was coming to his room, so that seems unlikely. Every instinct I had was warning me that he was a danger to me. So I ran away. I literally ran, into the hall, down several flights of stairs, through the lobby and down the Strand. To this day, I rate it as one of the best decisions I've ever made.

If he was just a sweet man who had a messy bathroom, he was no doubt offended and hurt by me being extremely rude. But at the time, I shouldn't have been weighing that up. I made a split-second choice that something was off, that my comfort was more important than his feelings, and left – and I made the right decision. The most shocking thing about this story, telling it half a decade later, is that I considered risking my safety so that a complete stranger would not think me rude for letting him buy me cocktails and then running away.

Safety

Sometimes not being rude is about protecting yourself, and while I will preach the virtues of complaining about bad service, telling your friends to piss off and shouting back at bosses who demean you, all of this advice comes with a honking great caveat, and that is to keep yourself safe. It is never stupid to err on the side of caution, and in any situation where you fear that being rude might lead to something dangerous it is perfectly legitimate to say you've got a boyfriend, an early meeting or a Bible study group to attend rather than being honest about why you are rejecting a man.

Many of the men I've spoken to over the course of my life do not understand the underlying sense of fear that women walk around with every day. They are even offended by the suggestion that women perceive men as dangerous. But, despite the fact that most men are lovely and decent and would never hurt a fly, women are still fearful. We ask each other to message when we get home after a night out to make sure that no one got murdered between the pub and their house. We walk down the street with our keys between our fingers like a low-budget Wolverine. We constantly make choices based on trying to stay safe, not angering anyone who might hurt us, not finding ourselves in a dangerous situation.

Being attacked or murdered by a man you've offended is

not common, but it happens a lot more often than you'd think. At least 139 women in the UK were murdered by men last year. The 'reasons' for this (there are, of course, no valid reasons) are manifold, but in some cases women were killed because they spurned men's advances, the kind of 'rude' behaviour that I actively condone. As women we have a responsibility to try to build a better world for each other, and not teaching men to expect sugar-coated rejections is part of that; but you also have a much bigger responsibility to yourself – to stay safe and avoid danger.

In 2017 posters started appearing in bars and pubs all over London which read: 'On a date which isn't working out? Tinder or POS date not who they said they were on their profile? Do you feel like you're not in a safe situation? Does it all feel a bit weird? Go to the bar and #AskForAngela – the bar staff will know that you need some help getting out of your situation and will call you a taxi or help you out discreetly – without too much fuss.'

Critics called them infantilising, claiming they promoted a culture of female cowardice and vilified men. I presume those critics hadn't ever been on a really scary date. Yes, women should be able to say, 'You do not look like your profile picture and I'm going home,' and then stride away without a moment's hesitation. But we should also be able to go running alone at night, sleep with as many men as we like without judgement and take our full lunchbreak without our bosses raising an eyebrow. These are ideals. Things to work towards. They are not currently wholly realistic. Women operate pragmatically in line with their experiences, and as such they often need a trick, like asking for Angela, or having a friend 'call with an emergency'.

If you are the kind of woman who can say, half an hour into

a date, 'Actually this isn't going to work, I'll get the bill and wish you all the best,' then that is brilliant; but if you're not, you shouldn't for a second feel guilty. Most men are good, nice people who would never hurt a woman. But there are plenty who aren't like that, and, as has been pointed out many times, every woman knows someone who has been hit or assaulted by a man. Yet no one seems to know anyone who has done the hitting or assaulting.

Men go through life knowing that they've got a decent chance of defending themselves. Women move around in the world knowing that they are physically weaker than every second person they walk past on the street. It's a good thing we don't dwell on this, because it's honestly pretty terrifying. So, while I implore you to be rude, I implore you much more to be safe, and never to feel guilty about putting on a sugar-coated voice and saying you have a boyfriend when you reject a man. You shouldn't have to, but honestly sometimes it's just not worth the risk to do otherwise.

The right kind of rude: about dating

- You're not obliged to spare anyone else's feelings. Of course, being nasty for the sake of it achieves nothing, but if you're telling a lie to a stranger, ask yourself why.

- Just because someone is being abusive via an app rather than in person does not mean that you have to ignore it. Dick pics might be a punchline, but it's also cyber-flashing and steps are being taken to make it illegal. If someone keeps doing it, you're fully within your rights to contact the police.

- Sometimes, when you avoid being rude to someone you've been on a few dates with, you tell yourself that it's to protect their feelings, when realistically it's to avoid the awkwardness of an honest conversation. This is where you need to be rude for someone else's sake.

- Ghosting normally happens when you're trying to avoid rudeness. It's mean and it's not OK. Far better to explain that the chemistry isn't there than just go silent. Honesty is the right kind of rude – ghosting is the wrong kind.

- If you don't like someone romantically it is not nasty or unkind to be realistic about that. You do not need to keep seeing them for more dates to be sure about it unless you want to.

- No one 'deserves' your romantic attention. You do not owe anyone anything on that front.

- The exception to every rule when it comes to rude dating is your own safety. If it becomes a red-flag situation, do whatever you need to in order to be safe. The vast majority of men are not a threat, but the fear that women feel is not unfounded, and at the end of the day it's just not worth taking the risk.

Taylor Swift

Taylor Swift was born in 1989. She is a multi-award-winning, stadium-filling, multi-platinum-record-holding singer-song writer who, aged fourteen, convinced her parents to move from Pennsylvania to Nashville in order for her to focus on her career.

On the one hand, the cookie-baking, cat-loving Taylor Alison Swift is about as un-rude as you can get. She's about as sweet as Ben & Jerry's Chocolate Fudge Brownie. She invites her fans over to her houses to listen to her music and provides home-made baked goods. She loves her mum. She grew up on an actual Christmas tree farm. And yet, more than any other woman in the music industry, Taylor Swift embraces the power of rude when it comes to defending her rights as an artist and a creator.

In 2015, Apple Music decided that they would only pay artists for their music outside of the free three-month trial period for users. Taylor Swift publicly told them that they couldn't use her music unless they paid for it, and as a result Apple had to rethink their entire strategy and pay artists fairly.

In June 2019 Scott Borchetta sold his record label, Big Machine Records, to Scooter Braun. Which was unfortunate for Taylor because Scooter had publicly mocked her during the Kardashian-West saga of 2017. As a result, all the music that Taylor had recorded for Big Machine now effectively belonged to someone she hated – a bitter pill to swallow, given that these songs were a record of her life, her feelings and her emotional development from child to adult. Bitterer, even, given that this was all a result of a contract she signed when she was in her early teens. Many performers would privately have mourned the loss of their work and put on a smiling face, afraid of angering the people they had previously worked with. Not Taylor.

When the sale was announced, she released a statement which read:

> I learned about Scooter Braun's purchase of my masters as it was announced to the world. All I could think about was the incessant, manipulative bullying I've received at his hands for years.
>
>   Like when Kim Kardashian orchestrated an illegally recorded snippet of a phone call to be leaked . . . Or when his client,

Kanye West, organized a revenge-porn music video which strips my body naked. Now Scooter has stripped me of my life's work, that I wasn't given an opportunity to buy.

This is my worst-case scenario. This is what happens when you sign a deal at fifteen to someone for whom the term 'loyalty' is clearly just a contractual concept. And when that man says, 'Music has value,' he means its value is beholden to men who had no part in creating it.

Unsurprisingly, the men who sat behind the desks weren't pleased about Taylor taking the fight public. Some, most notably Braun's wife and his client Justin Bieber, came forward in support of Scooter and to deny that he was a bully. Five months later Taylor made another public statement, saying that she had exhausted all avenues of negotiation with them privately, and that Big Machine was trying to block her from performing a medley of songs *that she wrote* during the American Music Awards. She instructed her fans – who are in their millions, worldwide – to let Scooter and Scott know how they felt about this situation, and to pressure Scooter's remaining clients not to stand for his behaviour.

It was a move so ballsy that even I, the rude evangelist, took a sharp intake of breath when I read it. She was pulling literally no punches, putting the entire weight of her fame behind stopping these men from playing God with her work. And it worked. Big Machine allowed her to perform the work, and as of November 2019 she'll be free to record new versions of her older songs, which she'll own.

Similarly, Taylor seemed to grow tired of the narrative that she dates too much. Rather than putting up with it, she called it out, saying, 'If guys don't want me to write bad songs about them, they shouldn't do bad things.' In her 2019 album *Lover* she turned the double standard of male-female behaviour into an anthem which features the words, 'If I were a man . . . They would toast to me (oh), let the players play. I'd be just like Leo in Saint Tropez.'

We're not all like Taylor. In fact, none of us are. We don't have millions of fans, sold-out stadium tours and multiple houses. But women all over the world know what it feels like to watch someone else – usually a man – take credit for our work. Or to have our achievements overshadowed by our romantic status. How often, when that occurs, do you speak up, rather than simply allow it to happen?

Of course, as this book acknowledges, women who 'transgress' don't often get away with it. Taylor has been smacked down time and time again, by the press, on social media, by other celebrities, for her refusal to remain silent. There are, predictably, people all over the Internet commenting that it was her own fault for signing the contract so young, that she should shut up and get over it, that she's making a fuss about nothing. But that's the thing. Whether it is singing about boys who cheated on her, writing lyrics about friends who screwed her over, or taking on multinational corporations who don't want to pay her, Taylor has never been willing to keep her mouth shut – something that we could all emulate in our own lives. That's why her unflinching refusal to cave in to Borchetta and Braun is so important.

As Taylor Swift demonstrates, you don't have to choose between being a nice person and being a rude person. You can be both. Being rude doesn't mean being nasty. It means being honest, direct and responsible for your own wants and needs. Women all over the world are encouraged to play nicely, keep quiet and be sweet. Sugar and spice and all things nice. The options for women have always been ball-breaker or sweetheart. Taylor Swift refuses to play that game and proves that she can be both. She can bake gingerbread while wearing a poloneck, send her fans gifts and use Tumblr to connect with the people who love her, but she can also shout down powerful men who want to prevent her from singing her own songs. She can be sexy and serious, hard and soft, beautiful and professional, rude and kind. And so can you.

CHAPTER FOUR

RUDE ABOUT SEX

Back in 2014, my friend Angelica Malin and I launched an online sex magazine called *About Fucking Time*. Our mission statement was very simple: good sex is a right, not a privilege. We launched the (now long defunct) magazine after spending our early twenties listening to our friends talking about their mediocre sex lives and arriving at the conclusion that something really had to change. Time and time again I have heard women say that they cannot orgasm, that sex isn't really for them, that they only like sex because it makes them feel close to their partner, or that they have sex when they don't feel like it because it's 'easier'.

If there is one place where being rude makes sense, it's in the bedroom. You strip away every other aspect of societal expectation. You're naked, touching each other, making noises and faces, tasting and smelling each other's bodies. There really shouldn't be any room for a fear of being rude – sex is the rudest thing two people can do. And yet there is.

Despite being the official flag-bearer for honesty during sex and demanding at least as much pleasure as you give, I understand why women opt for a Neville Chamberlain-style policy of appeasement during sex because I've done it myself.

When I was eighteen, I started a four-year affair with a man in his fifties. He was incredibly sexually experienced, and while there were other aspects of our relationship which weren't great, he was sexually very generous. However, I was nervous, self-conscious and struggled to reach orgasm as quickly as I thought I was supposed to. Porn had given me the impression that I should come in less than five minutes, and that anything longer was just plain wrong. So the first time we had sex, I faked it. And the thing about faking it is that once you start, you have to keep going.

I kept faking orgasms for six months. Occasionally I would allow myself a real orgasm, and he would comment on how much longer it had taken. Not with judgement, just with curiosity, making sure that I was OK, that he hadn't done something I didn't like. Of course I could have said something, but is there anything ruder than admitting to someone that you've been faking orgasms for literally years? That their kindly sexual efforts weren't good enough to bring you to climax?

I got it into my head that it was my fault, that I was too slow to orgasm, and therefore that orgasms should only take place during masturbation – in my own time. It seemed selfish (rude) to expect a man to spend twenty minutes helping me to come, and whenever I got close I would worry about how long I was taking and lose my groove. So I just skipped the whole party. It didn't occur to me that perhaps the person I was getting it on with wouldn't mind giving up twenty minutes of his life to make me come, which he almost certainly, with retrospect, wouldn't have minded. It also didn't occur to me that, as I'd spent a lot longer than twenty minutes giving blow jobs and hand jobs, I might deserve some reciprocal attention. Faking it seemed polite, so that's what I did.

Sex became a performance. The orgasm had to seem real, convincing and satisfying without being over the top enough to arouse suspicion. I used to boast at drinks with girlfriends that I was the Meryl Streep of faking orgasms.

Eventually I got older, ballsier and less generous in the bedroom. My fake orgasms went from Meryl Streep to Lindsay Lohan, and my boyfriend at the time realised what was going on. One day we were having sex, I was on top and I gave my faux climax a three out of ten on the effort scale. 'Darling?' he asked after we had finished. 'Was that . . . real?'

I dived face-first into the pillows and attempted to mask my bright-red face. 'No,' I said into the pillow. 'I faked it.'

'Why would you fake it?' he asked me. 'Has it happened before? How often?'

So, I did the rude thing and told him the truth. I'd faked the vast majority of the orgasms I had had with him. I also explained that I had done so out of guilt about how long it takes me to orgasm, stress of not performing properly and a desire to seem like I was good at sex. It was a painfully embarrassing conversation which I have not enjoyed reliving. But, after that, it got better. I stopped faking. I relaxed. Things got easier, and I learned the joy of having sex with someone when it's not a race to climax, but it's a probable outcome. And the grand irony is that, once I stopped worrying about how long it took me to reach orgasm, it got a whole lot quicker. Twenty minutes became five, and now I orgasm during sex almost as quickly as I do alone. I also realised that, even if you don't orgasm during sex, it's very reasonable to expect to have one afterwards.

My husband is the only person with whom I have never faked an orgasm. Perhaps that was a sign. But our gratifying sex life is at least, in part, due to my rudeness. In the very early days of our relationship, he once fell asleep immediately after we had had sex. I poked him in the ribs until he woke up and then fixed him with an incredulous look. 'Did you think we were finished?' I asked him.

'Um . . .' he replied.

'If you come, I come,' I said. A bit like Jack and Rose on the Titanic.

'Point taken,' he replied.

Six years later, I've never had to remind him again. I was less than delicate in expressing my outrage that he had fallen asleep without attending to my needs, and I left him feeling bad. Rather than feeling bad about it too, I tried to fight my guilt about having been honest. If someone else had done that years earlier, when he was first sexually active, I wouldn't have needed to say anything.

Tell the men with whom you are having sex that your orgasm matters. Point it out if they are not pleasing you sexually. Don't lie there with your legs open, letting someone prod at your arid clitoris or pull at your nipples because they are a nice person or because you think it's just part of having casual sex. It's not. There is no point in having sex unless you are going to enjoy it.

Faking it

I used to claim that faking an orgasm was a perfectly reasonable way to bring a sexual encounter to an end. Sometimes you just know that you're not going to get there, and you want the whole thing to come to a nice, gentle finish so that you can go to sleep. There was a time where I vehemently defended it. But, let's face it, it's another lie we tell to avoid being rude.

It's perfectly legitimate to say to the person you're having sex with, 'It's not happening for me tonight, shall we stop?', or, if you're feeling generous, 'I'm not going to come but I'd love it if you did.' Neither of those sentences is unkind or unreasonable.

Faking an orgasm is just like telling a man in a bar that

you have a boyfriend. It places a value on sparing the man's feelings, rather than being honest about your own. And unless you have a good reason to protect that man from the truth, then you should say it. There would be far fewer men in the world who are bad in bed if we all started being honest about how much or how little we enjoyed sex with them.

At university I slept with a friend who, after he rolled off me, said, 'Wow, you came like what, eight times?' I had not had one single orgasm, nor had I pretended to. Someone along the way had given him a very confused impression of what an orgasm was, which meant he was now going around having mediocre sex and thinking he was the orgasm fairy.

It's OK to do whatever you want during sex as long as it's between two consenting adults. But if you fake an orgasm to bring sex to an end, at least ask yourself why you decided to put on an ego-boosting show rather than tell the truth.

The orgasm gap

A study published in the *Archives of Sexual Behaviour* in 2017 found that straight women have fewer orgasms with their partners than any other group. Unlike lesbian women, who reported always or almost always achieving orgasm during sex, women with male partners only reported having orgasms 65 per cent of the time; 95 per cent of men, on the other hand, reported that they always or almost always orgasm during sex.

Here are some other (quite depressing) facts about the female orgasm, from a 2017 Family Planning Association study:

- Over 80 per cent of women could not reach orgasm through intercourse.

- Most women (72 per cent) reported difficulty in achieving a simultaneous orgasm with their partners.
- About one in seven women experienced pain during orgasm.
- Almost 3 per cent of women had never had an orgasm.

And from Public Health England in 2018:

- 42 per cent of women would describe their sex lives as 'unsatisfactory'.

Isn't that just brilliant? Almost half of us are having sex which is unsatisfactory.

It might sound a bit dramatic, but unsatisfactory sex subjugates women. When we lie back and think of England, we put sex at the bottom of a long list of things that we as women do as emotional and physical labour. According to the Office of National Statistics, women do an average of 60 per cent more hours of unpaid work in the home every week than men. So, when you allow your partner to have bad sex with you because you don't want to hurt his feelings or reject him, then you're adding yet more hours to your running total. Plus, you're reinforcing the status quo. The more your partner thinks that the kind of sex you are having is acceptable, the less likely he is to change. And there you are, trapped in a cycle of unsatisfactory sex with someone who might even believe you are enjoying yourself.

Sex should be fun. It should feel good, make you feel even better and bring you closer to the person you're sleeping with (unless that's not what either of you want). Sex should never, ever be a chore. And if you learn to be rude about it, it won't be.

In 2019, when I was running the *Grazia UK* website, I asked the women who worked for me to tell me their most controversial opinion as part of a features meeting. They ranged from the amusing to the bizarre. A writer named Georgia Aspinall told me, 'I think penetrative sex is a scam.' We all laughed, but when she wrote the piece I realised how cripplingly right she is. Unless you're trying to get pregnant, there really isn't anything essential about being penetrated with a penis. You can orgasm without it, you can use toys to simulate it, you can still enjoy a mutually gratifying sex life with your partner without it. Most women don't orgasm from penetration anyway. The fact that we say 'sex' and think 'penetration' perfectly demonstrates how the conversation about sex ignores women's pleasure. While I'd never tell anyone else how to run their sex life, I have taken Georgia's advice and slightly refocused my own to include more sex which is about mutual enjoyment and less obsessed with penetration.

Lots of us enjoy the closeness of penetrative sex, but for instance, if you go home with a stranger for a one-night stand, there is no obligation to actually have 'sex' in the traditional format. If you want to, and if you are clear about your desires, you can do everything but (like when you're a teenager, but to a much higher standard). That way you get all the pleasure without running any of the risks.

Saying no

There is a very old, very incorrect view that men like sex more than women do, that men enjoy sex and that women provide it as a service. For the avoidance of doubt, and the demolition of stereotypes, a 2019 study of 2,000 people by Illicit Encounters, an extramarital dating website, found that 43 per cent of women said they had a higher libido than the person they're sleeping with, while 42 per cent of men said the same thing. So, on average, we're all as horny as each other.

Anyway, the idea of women not liking sex has long, complicated roots in history, politics and religion. Suffice to say, it was convenient to create a myth that women do not like or want sex and that men need to trick, convince or bribe them into having it. Girls, on the other hand, were told to keep their legs shut, never take a taxi home with a man and expect to spend their premarital life rebuffing advances from cads, aiming to cross the finishing line of their wedding still *virgo intacta*.

Women were taught to say no if they weren't married. However, they were rarely taught that they were allowed to say no after marriage. Shockingly, until 1991 marital rape was not a crime. So sex between a married couple, even if it was not consensual, could not be ruled as rape. Women weren't taught to say no to their husbands because sex was considered to be part of their wifely duty.

Even more depressingly, a 2018 YouGov survey of 4,000 people commissioned by the End Violence Against Women Coalition revealed that one in four Britons believed that non-consensual sex within marriage did not constitute rape.

If *The Power of Rude* teaches you anything at all, it should be that you have the exclusive right to decide what happens to your body. Your husband or boyfriend doesn't have a right to your body, however long you have been together, how close you are as a couple, how many times you have had sex before. It's strange that, as women, we are able to worry about how rejecting our partners might make them feel, and yet for some reason not expect them to worry about how unwanted approaches might make *us* feel.

Saying no to sex should have absolutely no emotional repercussions. It's a bit like offering each other another glass of wine, or asking whether they'd like to see the new James Bond film: if they say yes then that's lovely, you can share in it; if they say no then that's fine too – if you really want it, you can enjoy it on your own.

It's easy to understand why women don't reject their partner's sexual advances – because there's an underlying societal notion that after marriage a man has automatic, unfettered access to his wife's body; but this is legally, socially and emotionally wrong.

Even if you're not in the terrifying 25 per cent who believe that marital rape doesn't exist, there is still a stigma about saying no to sex when you're in a relationship.

Your partner rolls over, puts his hand on your chest and gives you a look, and if you don't automatically burst into flames of lust, you're a boring prude who hates sex and who'll probably end up being cheated on.

Part of the problem is the fact that we all think we're having more sex than we actually are. As part of a study on misperceptions, which became a book titled *The Perils of Perception*, the research agency Ipsos asked people in Britain and the US to guess how often men and women aged eighteen to twenty-nine in their country had had sex in the past four weeks. The study says: 'On average people think young women have sex twenty times every four weeks and the guess for men is slightly higher at twenty-two times. In fact, when asked in the survey, 18–29-year-old women and men report they have had sex five and six times every four weeks respectively.'

The perception that everyone else is constantly getting laid contributes to the pressure never to say no to sex. But the problem is that if you say yes to sex you don't want, the sex will probably be mediocre. Which makes you feel less inclined towards having sex next time, and probably makes your partner feel pretty rubbish too. If instead you stop worrying about being rude, say, 'Not tonight darling,' and wait until you're feeling really horny to jump your partner's bones, then your sex life will improve. Stop measuring how great your sex life is by how often you do it and start measuring it by how satisfied you are and how much fun you're having.

Cruel to be kind

When I started sleeping with my husband, who had been in a long-term relationship prior to me, I quite quickly realised that he still had a sex routine which was adapted to someone else's body. The entire thing was designed by two people and probably worked for them, but parts of it didn't work for me, and the idea that he was applying someone else's likes and dislikes to me made me feel faintly uncomfortable.

Had I been sensible I would have said, 'I don't like the way that feels,' or 'Could you do that more gently?' But instead I tried time and time again to give him non-verbal cues. I'd wiggle in one direction for yes and another for no. Make noises like I was trying to give him echo location. But in the end, I realised that it wasn't going to work. He was not magically going to guess – especially as we'd only been sleeping together for a couple of weeks – what I wanted. So I said it in words. It was embarrassing and hard, and I felt like an ungrateful bitch, but I told him everything he was doing that didn't work. And I did it using a classic management tactic: you give a compliment, then a criticism, then another compliment.

Being rude doesn't have to mean being nasty. It's perfectly direct enough to say: 'I love it when you kiss my neck, but when you bite me it makes me feel uncomfortable.' Of course, there is nothing wrong with being totally blunt – as I said before, when you've seen each other's arseholes there's really no need to be coy – but this is about finding the level of rude that is comfortable for you. If you need to feed someone a compliment sandwich in order to say the rude thing you've been avoiding, you do. Baby steps and all that.

Caroline, forty-one, told me that she spent several months putting up with bad sex:

> I really liked the guy I was dating, and he was absolutely lovely. But he was really not my type in bed. I didn't say anything because I didn't want to upset him, and then one day after another really uncomfortable session I lost my temper and shouted: 'My clitoris is not a spelling mistake and your finger is not an eraser, why are you doing it like that?'
>
> Unsurprisingly, given that I'd spent the previous weeks moaning and sighing like I was enjoying myself, he was really upset. I do actually think that if I'd said it more gently, he'd have been fine with it, but as it was I knocked his confidence so badly that he struggled to get it up. We stopped seeing each other after that, and I still feel a bit bad about it.

Condoms, stealthing and the law

We discuss condoms more fully in the health chapter. Suffice to say, many men complain about condoms while many women find them a good and practical way to have safe sex (in fact they're the only way to have totally safe sex).

I've never understood the temptation to forgo the condom. Yes, it might feel better, but thinking you might be carrying the child of a man named Andre who, you're pretty sure, took £20 from your wallet on the way out doesn't feel great. Neither, I am reliably informed, does having to spend a day waiting at the GUM clinic because you've got a worrying itch. There's nothing morally wrong with an unplanned pregnancy or catching an STI, but if you can avoid either of them then you might as well. And yet, despite the very solid logic for using condoms, men will fight to avoid them.

One of my first experiences of being rude during sex was when I was at university. After a drunken party I fell into bed with a very attractive and very rude guy whom I quite fancied. Before we started having sex, I handed him a condom. 'Do we have to?' he asked. 'I don't have anything.' He didn't even ask if I did. For all he knew I could have been riddled with previously undiscovered vaginal woes. 'Yes, we do,' I insisted.

The sex was fine – nothing to write home about – but then a little way into the drunken fumbling I noticed him starting to take off the condom. 'I'm sorry, what are you doing?' I asked, too genuinely shocked to mind my manners.

'It's annoying me,' he told me. I got another condom from the bedside table and handed it to him. Begrudgingly he put it on. Later the same thing happened; I saw him reaching to take off the condom, and only when I looked him in the eye and said, 'You know I'm not on the pill?' did he keep the damn thing on.

I should not have had to terrify a man with the prospect of fathering my child in order for him to keep the condom on. I also should have felt, the moment he tried to take off the condom, therefore taking us from consenting condom sex to non-consenting unprotected sex, that I could tell him to get fucked. But I didn't. A big part of me (though I wouldn't have admitted it to myself at the time) was flattered that he was interested in sleeping with me – grateful for his interest. And on top of that I felt I was being boring for forcing him to wear a condom, a big killjoy who wasn't cool or adult enough to be on the pill. So I didn't tell him that it was inappropriate to try to remove the condom. I didn't shout down his total lack of respect for my boundaries. I waited until he had his orgasm and he'd assumed I'd had mine (I had not), and then tried to sleep in a neat and delicate way so as not to disturb him.

Many, many women have experienced men trying to remove a condom during sex – something that they presumably see as naughty and pushing their luck but not morally wrong. However, in some countries, Sweden for instance, it is illegal. It's the reason why Julian Assange is wanted there for trial.

The *Columbia Journal of Gender and Law* published a paper in 2017 titled 'Rape-Adjacent: imagining legal responses to non-consensual condom removal', in which the act is described as arguably an assault:

> Non-consensual condom removal during sexual intercourse exposes victims to physical risks of pregnancy and disease and, interviews make clear, is experienced by many as a grave violation of dignity and autonomy. Such condom removal, popularly known as 'stealthing', can be understood to transform consensual sex into non-consensual sex by one of two theories, one of which poses a risk of over-criminalization by demanding complete transparency about reproductive capacity and sexually transmitted infections. Adopting the alternative, preferable theory of non-consent, this Article considers possible criminal, tort, contract, and civil rights remedies currently available to victims. Ultimately, a new tort for 'stealthing' is necessary both to provide victims with a more viable cause of action and to reflect better the harms wrought by non-consensual condom removal.

For the avoidance of doubt, tampering with the agreed contraception that you and a partner are using is not only immoral and, in some countries, illegal: it could also be argued to be rape under UK and US law. In 2017 Dr Sinead Ring of the University of Kent told Stylist Magazine: 'A lot comes down to what can be proved in court . . . if it's proved the woman consented to sex with a condom and he changed the circumstances under which she'd consented, it's quite possible he'd be convicted of rape. But a jury would have to determine that he didn't have a reasonable belief in consent and just went ahead and did it anyway.'

Given how low conviction rates are in general it's understandable that women aren't keen to attempt to prove that a condom was removed by the male party without consent. I know I wouldn't have considered for a moment taking my one-night stand to trial, or to the police, over a shitty act of bad behaviour that he almost certainly believed to be permissible.

What I should have done, and what I would do now that I'm older, tougher, meaner and less worried about making people like me, is to have told him afterwards that taking the condom off wasn't OK. Instead of letting him have the entire duvet and trying to sleep with one freezing leg, I should have said to him, 'Did you know that what you did just then is actually classed as sexual assault in some countries?' Because that way he would have gone out into the world fully and unquestionably aware that what he did wasn't OK. And hopefully, if he were a decent person, and I really didn't know him well enough to say whether or not he was, it would mean that he never did it again.

Should it have been my job to educate him? Of course not. But we have to deal in realities, not ideals. And the reality is, every time we are polite when we should be rude, we send a message that everything is OK. We condone a person's actions when we don't call them out. So, because I wasn't rude to that guy, I sent the message that his attempts at stealthing were just

'Jack the lad', boys will be boys, naughty but nice. When in fact they put us at risk of becoming parents before we'd reached our twenty-second birthdays and violated the agreement that we had made.

Anal, facials and kink

The British Sexual Fantasy Research Project of 2016 claims that 62 per cent of Brits have had a fantasy about being either dominant or submissive in the bedroom. They also found that around 2.2 million of us admitted they'd had violent sexual fantasies. One in five women between the ages of twenty and thirty-nine had anal sex in 2010, and 46 per cent have tried it at least once, compared with just 33 per cent in 1992. In short, we're increasingly a nation of kinky bastards. And that's absolutely fine. As long as it is consensual.

Unfortunately, that isn't always the case. Over and over again I speak to women who've gone home with guys after dates, absolutely expecting sex. But not the kind of sex they get. Instead of a bit of a romp, without any negotiation or discussion the guy they're with tries to spank them. Or wants to have anal sex. Or slaps them across the face. Or chokes them (something you really shouldn't try unless you've done the research first).

The intention might be sexy, and there's no shame at all in wanting to have rough or kinky sex, but without prearranged negotiation you've basically taken a woman home with you and then smacked her about. There are plenty of people who, reading about this unplanned spanking or men who push for anal, would simply say that the woman in question should give a firm no, pick up her knickers and head for the door. Unfortunately, it's not always as easy as that. In the heat of the moment, saying no is hard. And in an age of porn, when these previously super-kinky activities are considered totally normal, it's easy to feel that you're a big, boring prude for preferring a man to come inside you rather than on your face while holding a hunk of your hair.

Every time I've had a man do something to me sexually which I wasn't in the mood for, or that I judged a bit risky, I know they would have stopped if I'd told them to. I've often had sex where there has been a safe word for that exact purpose. But the thing is, saying the safe word (or in more normal sex, just saying, 'I don't think I'm up for that') takes huge confidence. It's rejecting someone when they're being vulnerable towards you, it's declaring yourself as not being up for specific sexual acts. Sometimes it kills the mood. Which is why so many of us have put up with being fish-hooked or painful anal sex.

Acts which can be gratifying when you find them enjoyable are abusive or degrading when you don't. And yet we choose that degradation over the other, apparently less appealing option of saying: 'We didn't discuss doing this and it's making me feel uncomfortable, I'd like to stop.' Even in the moment when we're face down with our bum holes on display, we still cannot bring ourselves to be rude.

If you are going to have adventurous sex, you need to undertake a negotiation beforehand so that everyone is clear about their limits, even if it does feel a bit like that scene from *Fifty Shades of Grey*. If you struggle with using a safe word, you can use a 'safe motion' like balling your fists or shaking your head instead.

Sex out of politeness

As a result of the #MeToo campaign, a conversation started to emerge about the sexual grey areas. Women began to be open about the fact that they had had sex not through force, not even through coercion, but through politeness. Of the women who took the *Rude* survey, 58 per cent said that they had at some point in their life had sex out of politeness. Many respondents answered that they had done this many times; a few even said that they had sex out of politeness almost every time.

Back in 2017 I wrote an article titled 'Women are having sex out of politeness and that's got to stop'. It's one of the things I've been most contacted about in the course of my career. Hundreds of women messaged me to tell me that I wasn't the only one who had had sex out of politeness, sex I didn't want but could easily have avoided if I'd just said, 'Actually, really no thank you, I want to go home.'

My ultimate politeness sex story goes like this. In my late teens I went to dinner with a middle-aged couple I didn't know well. I had met them through a wider group of friends, and they were friendly, nice. The woman asked me to dinner and I said yes. She then sent me a long list of dates, therefore removing the option to claim I was busy, and somehow two weeks later I was sitting in their kitchen.

The wife made a curry. It was probably lovely, but way too hot for me (I have the palate of a small baby). Every bite I took hurt my mouth, but I didn't want to be rude. So I said nothing and ate it. They probably had Greek yogurt in the fridge. I could have just eaten the rice. There were easy fixes, ways to stop burning my tongue without offending anyone, but I didn't say anything. Because I didn't want to be rude.

After the curry, we went upstairs and had a threesome, also because I didn't want to be rude. I didn't fancy her much and I really didn't fancy her husband, but they'd been so nice to me, and I had sort of half known that it might happen. We'd flirted. Talked about being bisexual. Hints had been dropped – possibly even more explicit messages. I forget the exact details.

Anyway, while I'd enjoyed the flirting and maybe even liked the idea of having a threesome, when I got to it the situation didn't really appeal. Which was how I found myself lying on the bed, my eyes very tightly shut, trying to focus on the sensations that weren't unpleasant and reminding myself that this, like all things, would end. Telling myself that it would be awkward to ask them to stop, that I'd come this far so I might as well just get on with it. Afterwards I smiled a lot and said that I'd had fun. The woman told her husband to walk me back to the Tube with their dog, which he clearly didn't want to do. I lied and said I was going to get a taxi home.

Isn't that amazing? The man I'd just had a threesome with didn't really want to go out into the cold, so when his wife suggested he walk me to the Tube he honestly replied, 'I don't really want to.' He didn't toy with it, wrestle with it, struggle with it, he just said it.

The threesome wasn't a fun night, but it wasn't a traumatic experience either. I don't think of it that often. But I didn't enjoy it. And if I could go back in time and un-sleep with them, I probably would. I like to think that with ten years' more experience I would be able to mention before I arrived that I don't do well with spicy food, and that I would also have found the words to say I didn't want to have a threesome and wasn't on offer.

In compiling the research for *The Power of Rude* I found that the number-one answer to the question, 'What have you done because you didn't want someone to think that you're rude?' was 'had sex'. With strangers, friends, boyfriends, colleagues, employers, husbands, fuck buddies and pretty much anyone else you can imagine.

In the anonymous *Rude* survey, I also asked: 'Have you ever had sex out of politeness?' Fifty-one per cent of respondents said yes. Here are some of their comments.

'After a few years together, sex with my boyfriend became very painful, but I suffered through so he could have sex. It felt like I was being cruel by not having sex with him. In the end we did stop because it was too painful and we had bigger problems but I can still remember that sex because it was traumatic.'

'I would let my boyfriend have sex with me when I was still half asleep because it was the only way I could fit it into my schedule. I didn't want to admit that it did nothing for me, lest I hurt his feelings.'

'I've had sex out of politeness so many times.'

'I've found myself in situations where it was just easier to comply and have sex than to make a scene and leave.'

'Not sure I'd say out of politeness, but more in the sense it felt like a foregone conclusion. Like I couldn't be bothered to protest because it was more hassle than just having sex and complying.'

'I had sex out of politeness all the time with my ex-boyfriend, who had a much higher sex drive than me (and who wasn't good in bed).'

'It was horrible.'

The right kind of rude: about sex

- Faking an orgasm is a personal choice. You should not feel guilty about faking, or about refusing to fake. Instead you should choose whichever serves your own purpose best and roll with it.

- However, in a long-term relationship, if you're not enjoying sex you need to have that conversation. Sex should not be a service that you are providing for another person.

- Only a tiny, tiny percentage of women are actually incapable of orgasming. If you are struggling you might need time, a change of tack or to double down on your efforts solo. Don't just accept that you don't come and live without orgasms.

- By the time you're getting naked with someone, you should be comfortable enough also to be able to tell them what you want or need in the bedroom.

- Having sex doesn't have to mean penetration. You can set the boundaries about who puts what where, and those boundaries can be different every single time.

- You are never, ever obliged to have sex with another person unless you want to. You can be as rude as you like in order to ensure that it does not happen.

- As the person who will initially bear the brunt of contraceptive failure, contraceptive choices are up to you. If the person who you are having sex with objects to using a condom, then you should object to sleeping with him.

When given the choice between sex with a condom or no sex at all, the choice is usually quite an easy one.

- If you change your mind partway through a sexual encounter, you're perfectly within your rights to get up, put your clothes on and leave. No one else's right to have sex is more important than your right to choose whom you have sex with and when.

- Masturbation remains healthy, enjoyable and even important when you are in a relationship. Do not throw out your toys to please someone else. Secure men are not intimidated by vibrators, and insecure men have no right to get between you and your Rampant Rabbit.

- You don't owe anyone access to your body. Ever. It doesn't matter who they are, what the circumstances are. If you don't want sex, you don't have sex.

Anne Lister

Anne Lister (1791–1840) was a diarist, businesswoman and lesbian. In 1826, following the death of her uncle, James Lister, Anne inherited a property in West Yorkshire called Shibden Hall. In the 1800s the idea of a woman running an estate, particularly dealing with the finances and collecting the rents from tenants, was almost unthinkable. And yet Anne did it – with great success. While she is perhaps most famous for her lesbianism and the four million words of diaries she wrote, she was an impressive businesswoman and didn't let fears of societal standards or expectations restrict her ability to do battle with fellow industrialists.

According to Helena Whitbread, who deciphered many of Anne's diaries, which were written in a complex intellectual code,

> the challenge of managing the estate in such a way that it would both maximise her income and be passed on to her heirs in an improved condition was one which Anne took very seriously.
>
> Her entrepreneurial flair, her acquired knowledge, over the years, of mathematics, geology and engineering and her sharp negotiating skills with her male business rivals made her a formidable businesswoman in the newly emerging world of industrialisation, as is indicated in the following exchange with her defeated rival in the fight for selling coal in the area.

Anne wrote in her diary: 'Mr Rawson said he was never beaten by ladies & I had beaten him. Said I gravely, "It is the intellectual part of us that makes a bargain & that has no sex, or ought to have none."'

Much is made of Anne's sexual adventures, which were, admittedly, impressive, varied and staggeringly modern – she even had the equivalent of a marriage to another woman. There is no question that her commitment to living a sexually authentic life was brave in the extreme and raised a middle finger to the expectations of society. Yet it is well documented that Anne was subjected to harassment and abuse for her same-sex relationships, unusual style of dress and boldness in matters of business – a depressingly familiar concept even 200 years later.

Anne Lister is the perfect example of just how much you can get away with if you suspend your fears of being rude. If a woman who lived more than two centuries ago was able to ignore naysayers and build a successful business (much of which hinged on demanding money from men) without fear, then doesn't it follow that any of us should feel able to do the same?

Whether or not Anne was rude socially isn't clear, but I have no qualms in arguing that she was rude in general. From her diaries and her biographies it's pretty clear that Anne did not give a fuck what anyone thought of her: she had tons of affairs, called a woman she considered sleeping with 'new money' and must, unquestionably, have been pretty ballsy in order to keep control of her estate. In totally disregarding any concerns about being perceived as rude, Anne was able to enjoy a wide and varied sex life, a booming business and a fearsome reputation, all before the invention of electricity.

She is a testament to just how much we can get done if we stop wasting time worrying what people might think of us.

CHAPTER FIVE

RUDE ABOUT WEDDINGS

If you want to see a woman in her late twenties or early thirties lose the will to live, ask her to add up how much she has spent on attending other people's weddings in recent years. The light will drain out of her eyes as she mentally tots up just how much of her hard-earned cash has gone on a dress, a nice headband, a train ticket, a taxi from the station, drinks from the cash bar and a bloody present for the couple, who are already having an enormous party and then going on the fanciest holiday of their lives so far.

It is a truth universally acknowledged that between the ages of about twenty-six and thirty-six, you will spend the majority of your summer and your salary travelling to remote bits of the UK and paying through the nose to sleep in a questionable Airbnb because your boyfriend's work friend is getting married, your cousin is getting married, a girl you went to college with is getting married. The list goes on and on.

Lots of us find that the first couple of weddings we attend are exciting because they're gloriously novel, but by the time we've been to a few per summer, the joy is gone. I, on the other hand, love weddings because I'm rude: I haven't spunked all my nuptial goodwill on going to every single wedding in the Western Hemisphere and bankrupting myself in the process.

I used to write a column called 'Modern Etiquette', where people would get in touch with questions such as: 'I got period blood on someone else's sofa, what do I do next?' The vast majority were wedding-related, because weddings dominate so much of our free time and eat up so much of our income. There is a sense that, because it's someone's wedding, their wants and needs have to come first, even if that means you run out of holiday, put strain on your credit card or pay through the nose to do activities that make your toes curl.

This chapter started life as a little note in the friendship section, but the more I wrote the more it became clear that weddings are one of the areas where we all need a kick up the arse in learning to be rude, because it's totally possible to protect your annual leave and life savings without being a bitch.

If you're wondering where to start in terms of trying out the power of rude, then the next wedding invitation you receive is the number-one perfect opportunity.

Saying no

The stiffy drops onto your doormat, and whereas once you'd have been excited at the prospect of a weekend away, it now comes with a healthy side order of dread. Rather than putting it on the mantelpiece and looking at it with a glower of resentment every day for three months, do something revolutionary. Decide if you actually want to go. If you're sure you don't want to go, then RSVP no.

It's easy to think that because weddings tend to be planned a long time in advance, you can't say no. This is bollocks. It's an invitation, not a summons (this is a catchphrase very popular on Mumsnet). Just because you have been invited to a wedding does not mean there is an obligation to RSVP yes. So many of us take one look at the invitation, sigh, moan and put it in the diary. You do not have to do that. You do not need an excuse. 'No' is a complete sentence, and if the invitation comes from someone you don't like enough to want to watch them get married, then it doesn't really matter if they're a bit miffed that you won't be attending their special day. Though, to be honest, if they're significantly bothered about your RSVP then they're clearly not that diverted by the whole 'happiest day of your life' thing. 'Dear Karen, thank you for your very kind invitation, sadly I won't be able to join you, but I'm wishing you every happiness.' Bam. Saturday, 1 June is now yours to watch Netflix and pluck your toe hairs, all because you were bold enough to be the right kind of rude.

All of this is easier said than done. I have a horrible tendency and large-scale personal failing, in that I will say yes to an invitation, assuming that I will be more open to the idea of going closer to the time. Of course, that is complete bollocks. If an event is unappealing the day you receive it, it will still be unappealing down the line. My truly charming habit is to dread said event, worry about it, wait until it gets really close and then pretend to be ill. This is the wrong kind of rude. It's thoughtless, it puts other people to trouble, and it leaves me feeling horribly guilty. All in all, to be avoided. (For clarification, I have never done this at a wedding, though I have been sorely tempted.)

If you do want to go to the wedding (or any other social occasion), then work out how much you're willing to spend on it. It's OK that you probably have a different budget in mind for a close friend's wedding in a lovely location than for your third cousin's handfasting in Bognor Regis. The bride and groom are never going to know that you did a cost-benefit analysis about going to their special day, but you've got limited time, money and energy to spend, so you can't be wasting those precious resources on something that isn't going to make you happy and might make you miserable.

Presents

One of the first weddings I ever attended was quite a lavish affair for a couple who had plenty of money. The day before the ceremony I remembered, with a gut-twisting panic, that I hadn't bought them a present. Of course, when I logged on to their registry the only things left were disgustingly expensive. I was earning minimum wage as a receptionist and I almost cried as I spent a day's pay on a bathroom bin for them. Why? You probably know the answer by now. I didn't want to be rude.

It's not rude to keep your spending within a comfortable limit. You did not choose to invite yourself to the wedding, nor did you force the happy couple to cater steak for 100 people. Therefore, it is not your responsibility to offset their costs for the wedding via gifting. If you want to buy a present, then that's lovely. But if it's going to cause you stress, make your life harder or put you into debt, then absolutely fuck that. Your friends do not need copper-topped salt and pepper grinders more than you need to be able to pay your electricity bill.

Plus-ones

The only thing more annoying than travelling halfway across the country to eat a mass-produced roast dinner in celebration of someone else's relationship is doing it alone. If you've got a plus-one, then you can at least split the cost of a hotel room and have a glorious bitch about the bridesmaids' dresses after the whole thing wraps up. Of course, the person throwing the wedding might not want to give you a plus-one. From a bride and groom's point of view, unless they know both halves of the couple equally well, a plus-one is a waste. They're paying for dinner and drinks for a complete stranger. Which is why you often find that you're invited to a wedding solo. The 'no ring, no bring' policy is massively popular – even Kate and William employed it for their royal wedding, which probably had more to do with space limitations than cost. But anyway, the wedding plus-one policy is largely based on how serious you and your other half are, and if you're single then you can dream on. Which, if you think about it, makes no sense at all. If the bride and groom don't know some of the other partners, then why does it matter whether your plus-one is a romantic attachment or just a friend of yours?

It would be rude to tell the happy couple that you'd only like to attend if you can bring a plus-one, but it's also kind of rude that you're only allowed to bring a guest if you're in a long-term romantic relationship. Of course, if it's a huge wedding full of people you know and love then it's fine to go solo, but if you only know a handful of people, isn't it worth being rude and asking permission to bring a guest, thus circumventing a situation where you spend £400 to make forced conversation with demi-strangers? The bride and groom would be totally within their rights to deny you a plus-one because they don't have the space or budget. You would be entirely within your rights to decide that if you don't have a plus-one, you don't need to go.

A word to the wise: if you're going to have this conversation, especially in a world where being honest about your feelings is still quite a new concept, it's better to do it face to face. When we discuss things in writing, all the nuance is lost and the tone disappears. You can't read a reaction and temper the strength of your phrasing to meet the needs of the room. It's why arguments online or by email are so much more toxic than face to face. Telling your friend to her face, 'I'm so happy for you, but it's a lot of money and annual leave to come and sit on my own at the singles table,' is unlikely to go down as badly as a WhatsApp message saying, 'I'm only coming if I can bring someone' will.

Also, it's much harder to say no to someone's face. Saying no to an email just means typing whatever you want to say, hitting send and then slamming your screen shut and pretending nothing happened. Whereas looking someone in the eye and telling them that they can't have something they want is far, far harder.

Knowing this was true, for a long time I made requests via email or message, so that anyone who said yes to me was doing so because they really wanted to. Which is admirable, but not very effective. If you want something that someone isn't keen to give you – time off work during a busy period, a salary raise, a plus-one at their wedding – and you believe that they should give it to you, then you should back yourself. This applies across the board, not just to asking for a plus-one. Whether you want a favour, a pay rise or pretty much anything else in life, ask for it in the way which is most likely to produce the result you want.

It's something that I still struggle with and still feel guilty about. I, like a lot of women, consider my wants and needs to be less important than everyone else's and therefore have to fight my tendency to self-sabotage by making requests in a way which makes it easy for the answer to be no. But that's pointless. If you feel confident that a request is reasonable, then have the courage of your convictions and ask in a way which is most likely to get a yes.

Hen parties

I recently girded my loins and transferred £197 to another demi-friend, and as I typed 'Hen partaaay!' into the transaction description box I couldn't help wondering why I was paying a large chunk of my weekly living budget to travel halfway across the country to celebrate with someone towards whom I am (mutually) ambivalent. The difficulty about hen parties is that they entail handing over a large sum of cash and some of your annual leave, sometimes to a stranger, and hoping that they've got the same concept of a good time as you have. Best-case scenario: you have a brilliant weekend and it was worth the money. Worst-case scenario: you end up in the situation a friend of mine was in recently, who called her mum (who lives in Ealing), sobbing, and begging her to drive to collect her from a freezing-cold, teetotal house in north Wales where she was sharing a bed with a chronic snorer. Her mother declined to do the six-hour drive to pick her up and she (just about) survived by drinking heavily in private.

The average UK-based hen or stag do costs £494 to attend; abroad you're looking at £998. If you go to four in a year you've spent between £2,000 and £4,000. The average UK salary is £29,000. So you're paying between 7 and 14 per cent of your annual income on making flower crowns and pretending not to feel uncomfortable about the butler in the buff.

Hen party policy is much the same as wedding policy. Don't say yes unless you actually want to go, and if you do actually want to go, make sure you can afford it. Don't get yourself into debt or leave yourself in financial stress in order to drink warm Prosecco and play pin the cock on the poster. No decent friend will resent you for saying you can't afford to attend, especially if you're open about why. As will be discussed in the money chapter, the desire to pretend that you can afford things is very often based on a bigger desire not to make anyone else uncomfortable by being honest about your finances. But if we all got a bit better about admitting it when something is too expensive for us, then we'd all be able to do it more often and this whole 'emperor's new clothes' effect would be overcome.

Bridesmaids

Picture the scene. Your newly engaged friend asks you to meet her for a drink at an expensive cocktail bar quite a long way from your house. When you arrive she hands you a coloured cardboard box and inside is a balloon reading, 'Will you be my bridesmaid?' It's happened. The person you once loved has been invaded by Pinterest and Instagram bridal motifs. She is no longer the friend you want to spend time with. She is now a semi-sentient being who lives to plan her wedding and expects you to care about her nuptials as much as she does. Which is hard, because you probably can't imagine caring about your own wedding as much as she wants you to care about her napkin choices.

Bitching about being a bridesmaid is pedestrian and obvious, and yet almost impossible to resist. It's not the bride's fault that she's obsessed about the party she's throwing – she's spending her money and every second of free time in the year leading up to it trying to make it lovely. But the question is, are you on board to make that dream happen?

When I wrote my etiquette column, the single most repeated question was whether or not you can say no to being a bridesmaid. Whether it's because the person you've asked is too new a friend for you to feel comfortable about it, or because you've already done it so many times that the sight of a Ghost slip dress in muted pastel silk makes you want to throw up, the answer is yes. You are allowed to say no to being a bridesmaid. And if you want to say no, you should. It is a far, far, far better thing to say no when you're asked than to say yes and do a sub-par job. Friendships can be ruined by saying yes to being a bridesmaid when you wanted to say no.

Carrie, thirty-four, didn't say no to a bridesmaiding gig and lived to regret it:

> She was a really nice woman from my book club, and I liked her a lot, but we weren't close. I was surprised to be asked but flattered. I hadn't been one many times, so I wasn't really aware of how much work it was going to be. She wanted an elaborate hen do with multiple strippers, a classy sit-down meal and then a night out in a club, but she wanted it to cost no more than £50 a head. I did my absolute best, but I'm an accountant, not a wizard, and I could tell that she thought I was failing. In the end I got pregnant and told her that I wasn't going to be able to do both because I was tired and needed to look after myself. Which was mostly true. It went down really badly. At the wedding there was lots of 'Is that her?' from her other friends. I sent her a stupidly over-generous present to try to make up for it – but honestly, I should have just had the courage to tell her at the start that I had a child, a job and no time to help her plan.

Saying no might be badly received at the time, but dropping out of your bridesmaid role halfway through the wedding planning will go down a whole lot worse.

Bridezillas

When I was planning my wedding, my husband and I got into a routine. On a Saturday morning we would get in the car and drive to the florist, the wedding planner, the cake baker, whomever. We would scream at each other for the entirety of the car journey (me because I felt that he didn't care about what type of candles we were having, him because he felt I should pay more heed to speed limits on country lanes), then we would arrive at whatever wedding purveyor we had driven across the country to meet, I would check my lipstick in the rear-view mirror and we'd turn up at the front door holding hands and smiling. During the viewing or tasting or whatever it was we were spending our weekend doing, I would affect an air of sweet relaxation, as if I could hardly believe I was going to have a wedding at all, let alone make emphatic judgements about cake. 'What do you think, darling?' I would ask my husband every thirty seconds. I was determined not to be regarded as a bridezilla. It was the bridal version of 'I'm not like other girls.'

The one time that women are freely rude, demanding and specific in their wants is when they are getting married. Perhaps it's because we've been taught since childhood that this is the zenith of our experience. All of the normal rules which subjugate women seem to expire when we're planning our weddings. Bridezillas aren't born, they're made. But there's a reason why even the most grounded and down-to-earth woman can find herself roaring the words, 'It's my one special day and I want to feel like a princess.' Bridezilla behaviour is born of two things: repression and expectation.

I got married aged twenty-six, at which point I'd spent years suppressing my own desires, pretending that I didn't have strong feelings about where I went on holiday or what we had for dinner, saying, 'I don't mind which restaurant we go to' and then having crippling IBS because my pathetic body can't handle Indian food. But then I encountered the expectation that I was going to behave like a control freak because it was my wedding. Apparently, because I'd managed to hook myself a man, I was allowed to unleash all the finicky, irrational, gloriously selfish opinions that I'd been repressing since childhood. People who would have been shocked if I'd refused to go for expensive drinks on the other side of London on a Tuesday night were suddenly totally happy to indulge me when I cried over a rumoured peony shortage. It felt absolutely fucking great.

I look back at my wedding photos and see small details which would have been easy to fix if I'd been willing to tell the people who were being paid hefty sums that I wanted them adjusted. None of it really matters – it was without a doubt the happiest day of my life – but it's a testament to how foolish I was not to just embrace the punishing language aimed at women who transgress and style it out. It's unfair that the only time when women have society's blessing to demand perfection is when they're getting married, and only in the run-up to a single-day event. But it's a demonstration that it is possible.

Despite the fact that most women have never planned a large-scale event, every wedding I've been to has been a masterstroke of organisation almost exclusively created by the female partner. It's a testament to how much we are able to get done when we're freed from the shackles of expectation. When I see female friends turning into bridezillas, it fills me with joy. It's proof that we have it in us. When we feel that we have permission to be assertive, specific, demanding and selfish, we can create something incredible from a standing start.

The word 'bridezilla' belongs on the long list of words which are only ever applied to women, and it is of course designed to vilify women during a high-stress period of their life when they are (for the most part) putting together the wedding on their own.* But, beyond the snark of conflating 'bride' and 'Godzilla', I see the word as an enormous compliment. A bridezilla is a woman who has decided that if she's going to spend all her savings on a one-day-long party, she's sure as fuck going to have the correctly coloured tablecloths. The sad part about being a bridezilla is that a woman's ability to demand what she wants and make sure that she gets it applies only to the organisation of one day of her life.

The right kind of rude: about weddings

- Repeat to fade: 'it is an invitation, not a summons'. Just because you get a lot of notice about it doesn't mean you are obliged to go.

- Saying no doesn't mean you have to give an explanation. 'Thank you so much but we can't make it' is a full sentence.

- Weddings are supposed to be full of joy. It is far, far worse to go to a wedding with bad grace and resent being there than it is to RSVP saying that you can't come.

- Sometimes weddings are only fun if you can have a plus-one. You are not being selfish or horrible for saying that you want to bring someone, especially if you don't know anyone else who is going.

---

* According to WeddingWire.com, just 24 per cent of the total planning is done by the groom.

- If the bride and groom don't want you with your plus-one, that's fine too.

- Plus-ones are not just romantic partners. It is nonsensical to say that one person can bring someone they are sleeping with who doesn't know the bride or groom, but that another person can't because the relationship is platonic.

- Wedding blindness is a thing. The shutters come down and you forget that there is anything going on in the world. Sometimes you need your good friends to risk your wrath and remind you of that fact.

- Your wedding is a nice party and the start of a marriage, it is not the UN summit on ending climate change. Other people will care about your wedding around 5 per cent as much as you would like them to.

- The average wedding costs £391 to attend in total. That's a mini-break to a European country. Are you going to have more fun at this wedding than you would on a mini-break to Europe?

- You do not need to buy a new dress. Wear the dress you wore to the last wedding. No one else will remember what you wore unless you're very famous.

Sarah Churchill

Sarah Churchill, Duchess of Marlborough, Princess of Mindel-heim, Countess of Nellenburg (1660–1744) was an English courtier who rose to be one of the most influential women of her time through her close friendship with Queen Anne.

If you know much about Sarah, the chances are that you have seen *The Favourite*, a film about the complex relationship between Queen Anne, Sarah Churchill and Baroness Masham. While the film obviously wasn't a documentary, much of what it represented, at least in terms of rudeness, was accurate. Queen Anne was (like most monarchs) surrounded by people whom she paid and who were therefore unwilling to tell her unpalatable truths. British monarchs believed – possibly still do believe – that the ruling monarch was God's representative on earth. Therefore, telling off the king or queen was tantamount to telling off God. Add to that the fact that monarchs could have you banished, imprisoned or killed, unsurprisingly people weren't falling over themselves to call out problematic regal behaviour.

Sarah's skill as a courtier, aside from being witty and charming and clever and all the other things that courtiers were supposed to be, was that she was also direct, sharp and (you probably saw this one coming) rude. She famously didn't offer the queen flattery, and still referred to her by her childhood nickname, Mrs Morley. This was a sort of considered, constructive rudeness which worked incredibly well for the most part.

For several decades, their friendship flourished. Sarah Churchill was Mistress of the Robes and Groom of the Stool – the two highest positions that a woman could hold. Her husband, John Churchill, 1st Duke of Marlborough and hero of the Battle of Blenheim, was promoted and given £7,000 a year by the Crown, which is equivalent to £750,000 now. Plus, the queen gifted them Blenheim Palace, which has 2,000 acres and 187 rooms.

Unfortunately, Sarah's rudeness did not serve her so well for the rest of her political career, which is why she is included here. Eventually her cousin, Abigail Masham, pitched up at court and decided to take the opposite approach, opting to be flattering, supportive and kind to the queen at all times, regardless of what actually needed to be said or done. Unsurprisingly, this won her more favour than Sarah's brand of efficient political brutality.

Following a complicated spat over Queen Anne attending Abigail Masham's secret wedding, which honestly wouldn't be out of place in a 2020 WhatsApp group, Sarah fell further from favour and was eventually stripped of her roles. She and her husband left court, building came to a halt on Blenheim Palace and they retired instead to Germany. They remained abroad until the queen's death, at which point they returned to England.

Depressingly, not that much has changed since the 1700s, and as women trying to navigate the skill of being rude in the workplace, we still have to toe an invisible line through a complicated ballet of guesswork, intuition and hope. It's true that, like many of the other women held up as rude role models, Sarah is not exactly relatable. She died hundreds of years ago, was rich, an aristocrat and best mates with the queen. But beyond that, her life was – genuinely – much like yours or mine. She negotiated a workplace which was hostile to women, tried to balance complicated friendships and refused to sugar-coat her opinions or insights in order to make them more palatable to the people around her.

Sarah Churchill is included here because she was the opposite of what most of us are working with. She was, it's fair to say, rude beyond what was pragmatic and unable to read when she needed to rein in her ruder tendencies, but we would still do well to observe her skill. Her rudeness, tempered with astute political decision-making and charm, led her to be the second most powerful woman in the country, which at the time meant she was one of the most powerful women in the world. I'd say it's better to reach too high and fall from grace like Sarah did than to stay safely on the sidelines and achieve nothing at all.

CHAPTER SIX

RUDE AS A CONSUMER

You are most likely to need to learn to be rude, on a regular basis, as a consumer. It's no one's fault, but sometimes things go wrong. Products break, appointments are cancelled, the eyebrow threader slips and leaves you partially facially bald. The temptation, if you're not a fully paid-up member of the rude club, is to pretend that you are happy to have spent money on something substandard, and then go home and complain to people who can do nothing about the situation. We all know this is pointless, and it's time to stop.

The most experience I've ever had of people being rude – both in a positive and a negative sense – was when I worked at a very fancy London department store. We were required to wear suits and a full face of make-up, high heels and a smile, which hid the fact that the high heels were slowly lacerating our feet. Our job wasn't just to sell things, it was to make customers feel so special that they didn't resent how much money they had spent on something they could almost certainly have bought cheaper elsewhere.

There were two types of customers and, while I didn't realise it at the time, they would become the bedrock of my opinions about rudeness.

We had customers who were the right kind of rude: efficient, demanding and specific, with an expectation of excellence. They were firm but respectful. And then there were the other types: the ones who clicked their fingers or shouted, pushing and complaining just to be heard. The first type of rudeness was born of confidence. It came from people who knew how to shop in an expensive, pretentious store. The second type were the exact opposite. The customers who clicked their fingers and talked down to staff were the ones who secretly felt they didn't belong there, who didn't have the confidence to be calm, and desperately needed the people serving them to believe that they were important. It didn't seem to matter that these people were dropping £300 on a child's party dress or £200 on a pair of flip-flops. They needed us, the £9 an hour staff, to be impressed.

I understand why these people were intimidated. The first time my mother took me to Harvey Nichols (another, much cooler department store with even fancier stock), I walked through the handbag hall, scared to even breathe next to the McQueen and Chanel. All the beautiful women with huge hair and red lipstick were terrifying and I was convinced they were staring at me, assessing my outfit, and concluding that I didn't belong. My mother made short shrift of this. 'You've got just as much right to be here as anyone else,' she told me. 'Don't be silly. It's just a shop.'

Years on I still occasionally have to tell myself, 'It's just a shop,' 'It's just a bar,' 'It's just a party.' I've added my own little mantra now, which goes something like: 'They are at work, this is their job, they definitely don't care about you, they just want their shifts to be over so they can go home.' Sometimes, especially if you're an anxious person, it can feel like everyone is interested in your behaviour. Please believe me when I say that absolutely no one cares about your conduct as much as you do. No one is still thinking about that stupid thing you said last week or the way you opened that door.

In general terms, people do not care about you as much as you think (or fear) that they do, so it's pointless to waste time over-thinking.

Say please, say thank you, tip generously and ask for what you want, complain firmly but politely if you don't get it, say yes if you mean yes and no if you mean no, and then move on. Technically, it's that simple. The only other tiny step is unlearning everything else about rudeness that you've ever known.

Hair

If you are a woman who cares about her hair, the hairdresser is a sort of safe space. You arrive a bit ragged, and, as long as things go right, you can leave feeling like a new woman – utterly transformed. The magic of the hairdresser isn't really magic at all. For lots of women it's the only time when they sit quietly and read a book or play with their phone without being interrupted by a child, partner, work crisis or some other unavoidable irritation. Combine the magic of a couple of hours of selfish downtime with the transformative power of a really good blow-dry and the instant improvement to your general levels of polish that comes from a trim or some highlights, and you can see why lots of us look forward to having our hair done as if it's a demi-religious experience. Which is why it's a big deal when a haircut goes wrong.

When we talk about women's lives, we often do so in terms of moments, rites of passage and watersheds: our first kiss, first relationship, the first time we had sex – all of those are important. But I strongly maintain that there is another more significant 'first', and that's the first time a woman gets a bad haircut.

My first bad haircut happened when I was fourteen. I was a little chubby, carrying a very unattractive sunburn on my nose and generally convinced that I was hideous, as most of us are at that age. Previously I'd always had great haircuts which had left me feeling prettier, happier and more like myself. On this occasion, things were different. We've all been there. I said I wanted an inch off, the hairdresser insisted I needed far more than that. Intimidated, I agreed meekly and then felt that familiar sick feeling when the blow-dryer came out and my hair barely brushed my shoulders.

We all know that if a haircut is bad, wonky, not what you agreed or for any reason substandard, you're supposed to politely explain that you're not happy. Of course, I was fourteen and terrified, so this didn't occur to me. I paid and then cried all the way home, whereupon my mum gave me a big hug and welcomed me to adulthood. Crying after a trip to the hairdresser was, she told me, part of being a woman. Who among us hasn't said, 'I love it, thank you,' to a hairdresser while gulping back the tears and then ducked into a café bathroom to have a quiet sob in mourning for the hair that we've lost?

When you get a bad haircut, you're not just upset about your hair. You're upset about the time you lost getting it ruined, the missed potential to leave feeling happier and better about yourself. You're angry, frustrated, hurt and disappointed. It's a bitter cocktail of miserable feelings, and it might be a First World problem but it's a problem nonetheless.

Curly hair

As a white woman with straight hair I've had some hair disasters, but they're nothing like the experiences of some of the women of colour I've spoken to, who have had their hair butchered by people who didn't know how to cut curly hair. Maya, a twenty-nine-year-old writer, told me:

> I've only met three hairdressers in my entire life who know how to cut curly hair properly. Every other one I've been to does a terrible job, and I say thank you and pay the bill.
>
> At the end of the haircut the hairdresser always offers to blow-dry my curly hair straight, and I always say yes, even though I'd rather they did it curly. A couple of years ago a hairdresser used such high heat trying to get it straight that she burned the top of my head. All the skin peeled off, giving me super dandruff for a month. But obviously I still paid her and said I loved it.

In the first series of *America's Next Top Model* – every teenage girl's noughties delight – a woman named Ebony Haith was told she was going to have her head shaved for her 'makeover'. The white hairdressers brought in to do the head-shaving had no idea how to handle Ebony's African-American hair. The clip is agonising to watch: these women laugh at their own inability while they make a complete mess of Ebony's hair. Ebony herself, usually outspoken and confident, sits silently and seethes while they work, unable to find her voice to complain until after they've butchered her hair.

Knowing your rights

I've had four or five disastrous hair experiences since that first one, and only recently have I found my voice. I can honestly say that it is one of the most liberating things that has ever happened to me. Last year a colourist mixed up two tubes and ended up highlighting my light-blonde hair a dark-brown orange. I knew it had gone wrong, she knew it had gone wrong, everyone was on the same page. There was a time when I would have meekly accepted the terrible colour and paid to have it fixed. But, newly emboldened by the superpower of rudeness, I stood firm. I called the company I had booked the treatment through and demanded a refund, which I got. Then I returned to the salon, which had offered to fix the colour, and sat in the chair for eight hours while they made it marginally better. Then, rather than saying I was delighted and smiling, I took a big, deep breath and told them that it wasn't perfect, I wasn't happy, but I appreciated that they had tried to improve the situation. I've honestly never felt braver.

For what it's worth, you do not have to pay for a bad haircut. The Consumer Rights Act of 2015 states that services such as haircutting should be carried out 'with care and skill'. If your haircut has not been done with care or skill, you're within your rights to refuse to pay. Often the salon will offer to put things right, either with a different stylist or with someone more senior, but if you've got no confidence in the salon you can take your money elsewhere.

There is also a legal precedent for being compensated for a bad haircut. In 2017 a woman named Donna Smith won £9,000 in compensation after a £150 haircut. Of course, getting compensation or even just refusing to pay requires you to be honest about your experience. The Financial Conduct Authority estimates that around 15 million British people miss out on a refund by not complaining about services with which they were not satisfied, and on average that costs us each £275 per year.

Talking about hair is easily brushed off (ha ha) as flippant. Beauty is vapid and pointless, right? It's only hair. But I will forever stand by my opinion that the hairdressing salon is where we as women can learn to rid ourselves of the fear of being rude.

I've caught myself – many times – saying that the water temperature is absolutely fine when it's too hot or too cold. What have I achieved by doing this? The person washing my hair doesn't care. It's not a huge imposition to change the temperature of the water. They are asking because they want to get it right. And yet time and time again we put our own comfort below the convenience of a stranger who is being paid to provide a service, at absolutely no benefit to that stranger.

Is this a tiny problem in the grand scheme of things? Of course. But it's also a big fat fucking metaphor for the way in which we as women put our own wants, needs and comfort right at the bottom of the pile. The young woman who learns to say, 'Actually that's a little hot' or 'The towel isn't wrapped round my neck quite right' or 'There's a lot of shampoo in my ear' is going to grow into the adult who is able to say, 'I know you bought me dinner but I'm still going to call a taxi and go home,' or 'I've worked late every night this week and I need to leave on time this evening.'

Hair is not life or death. But that's why the salon is the perfect place to practise complaining. I can't help thinking that if someone had taught me to say, aged fourteen, 'Actually this wasn't really what I asked for and I'm disappointed with how it has turned out,' I might not have spent the next decade and a bit trying to work out how to shake off a pathological fear of seeming rude.

Restaurants

Hairdressing salons are where we first learn to complain (or perhaps not complain), but restaurants probably come second, because occasionally falling short of the expected standards is just part of the reality of running a restaurant. Sometimes food will be a little cold, under- or over-seasoned, or just not quite right. And for people who are fluent in the language of complaints, that's not a big deal. But, of course, for every one of us who can happily say, 'I asked for my steak rare and this is well done – I'd like another,' there are those of us who will chew our way through a beef bourguignon despite being a committed vegetarian, purely to avoid being rude.

Before I was a writer, when I worked as a nanny, I took my charge to McDonald's (I didn't say I was a very good nanny), where she had a Happy Meal. The meal was supposed to come with one toy but hers came with another. She opened it and was enormously disappointed. 'I wanted the one on the poster,' she told me. And to be fair, when you're seven that's quite a big deal. 'Can you ask?' she said to me.

Sensing that this was a teachable moment (and why be a nanny if not to nurture the feminists of the future), I said no, and instead offered to go the counter with her so that she could complain. She was nervous and could barely meet his eye, but politely told the man behind the till that she would like the toy advertised if there was one going, and he gave it to her. He even let her keep both. And in that moment, I swear she grew three inches. I didn't impart much wisdom to her during my tenure, other than that Taylor Swift is a queen, no matter what anyone says, but the singular gift I did give her was the ability to make a polite complaint. After that, whenever we went out to eat she would inspect the hot chocolate, cupcake or smoothie we'd bought and if (very occasionally) there was something wrong, she would quietly ask me, 'Can I complain?'

Of course, there were times – like when she told me that her teatime sausages weren't hot enough – that I regretted it enormously. But in the end, it was without question the most useful thing I did for her as her nanny. I taught her, before she had fully absorbed the message that women are not supposed to demand or even ask for things, that she had every right to make a polite and well-phrased complaint. Something that so many of us as adults still struggle to do.

I went to lunch with my mum recently, who happens to be an amazing cook and expert in all things food. She ordered a piece of fish called a ray wing, and a little while later a plate of something completely different arrived. After a bit of dithering, she called the waitress over and said: 'I'm so sorry, but I don't think this is ray wing.' The waitress assured her that it was ray wing and went on her way. My mother, who has cooked pretty much every piece of fish under the sun, silently fumed. She knew, without a shadow of a doubt, that she was right. And yet she didn't want to say anything.

At the end of the meal, when the waitress came back, we repeated the question: 'Are you sure that was ray wing?' Of course, the answer came back that it was indeed not ray wing, and that the plates had been mixed up on the way out of the kitchen.

First World problem? Of course. I doubt it was even the biggest catastrophe that happened in the restaurant that day, but it's a classic example of a woman ignoring her instincts and doing what she has been told, for fear of making a fuss. Doing it once over lunch isn't a big deal, but the thing is, it's not just once over lunch: it's every single time something is below an expected standard. It's every week, if not every day. It builds up to a lifelong habit of accepting the mediocre while paying for better.

Many of the people who took the *Rude* survey said that they hate complaining in restaurants because it feels like they're taking out their frustration on their waiter or waitress, who is usually totally blameless and often very badly paid.

This raises an interesting dilemma. If you go out to eat and the service is slow, the food is cold and the experience is generally underwhelming, it's not right that you should still end up paying full whack, or that you should have to eat food that you don't enjoy. For many of us, eating out is a treat and something we look forward to. It's not wrong to expect a certain level of care and quality. It's very noble to put up with bad food to spare the waiter, but it's also the same old problem – putting the needs of a stranger above those of your own for fear of seeming rude.

Lots of people who work in the food service industry are young, underpaid and not having the most fun day. So it can feel imperious, bordering on shameful, to summon said person to your table and tell them that the steak they brought over (which happens to cost more than their hourly wage) wasn't quite right. No one wants to be the bitch at table fourteen who snarls, 'Let me speak to your manager' to the teenage waitress who is only on her second ever shift.

But what's the other option? To sit and eat something of sub-par quality in order to avoid coming across as entitled? Not exactly a sensible option. Just like the hairdresser example, it's about making a choice to settle for something which isn't

OK in order to avoid a stranger thinking slightly less of you.

A few years ago, I spent the weekend in Cornwall with my husband and another couple. At dinner we ordered a bottle of red wine and a bottle of white, and I was asked to try the white. I tried it and, lo and behold, it was fizzy. It was not supposed to be fizzy. I told the waiter that the bottle was corked and that we'd like a different one – something I'd never done before in my life. To my surprise he shook his head. 'It's supposed to be like that,' he told me.

It wasn't supposed to be like that. I've drunk more wine in my life than I care to remember, and I know what should and shouldn't be fizzy. 'I don't think it is,' I told him. 'We'd really prefer another bottle.' 'I can get you another bottle,' he said, 'but it will taste exactly the same.'

At this point I started to lose my temper, and instead of being a mature adult and saying 'Yes, we'd prefer that,' I decided to announce that I was a professional wine taster and that the wine was off. For the avoidance of doubt, I am not a professional wine taster. My wine-drinking is strictly recreational.

The waiter, who couldn't have been more than twenty, looked a little surprised and duly brought another bottle. To my enormous relief (and it really was enormous), the second bottle was not fizzy, and we got on with the evening.

I was paying for that bottle of wine, and I'd been elected to try it. Those two factors should have been enough on their own to justify my request for a different, non-fizzy bottle. There was absolutely no need for me to claim that I was a professional wine taster. The point of this story is to illustrate that it's easy to lack the courage of your conviction when you complain, and a robust waiter who tells you that you're wrong might well be convincing, but the old adage is correct: the customer is always right.

You don't need to be a professional wine taster to know if a bottle of wine is off, nor an expert in Michelin-starred food to tell if a bowl of soup is too cold. You're paying for it, and if you don't think it's right then ask the question.

Allergies

Complaining about food that is late, cold or a bit meh is one thing, but surely it's easy to complain about food which could actually kill you? Apparently not.

Sophie has a moderate/severe allergy to avocado, among other things:

I went out for a group meal to a Mexican restaurant. It was very busy, the tables were heaving, so when we ordered our food I told the waiter about my avocado allergy but didn't make that big a fuss. The truth is, if I eat it I get a rash or hives on my skin, my lips swell up and I feel gross. Anyway, I asked for my meal without any avocado, and told the waiter that I'm allergic, but half an hour later my food arrived with avocado in it.

Everyone else started eating, and we were all starving. The waiter looked harassed, and I didn't want to make a fuss, slow down the evening or make trouble, so I just picked off the avocado and hoped for the best. Of course, I ended up having to go home because I was itching all over and my face swelled up and I missed the rest of the night. To add insult to injury, there was a supplementary charge for the avocado on our bill.

That night really showed me how important it is to be stronger in my convictions. Since then I've had a friend have a very near miss with anaphylaxis when a restaurant ignored her dietary requirements and she hadn't made a fuss about it. So now I tell them that I'm allergic and that it could be dangerous. Sometimes I feel like I'm making a stupid fuss, but it's just not worth running the risk. I could actually end up dying because I don't want to come across as rude.

An astonishing number of women have told me similar stories, when they've eaten things which give them IBS flare-ups, swollen lips or even meat when they are vegetarians to avoid making a formal complaint in a restaurant. I recently moderated a panel discussion with a group of women who had specific nutritional needs. One of them said, 'The rise of gluten-free was frustrating, because as a celiac I felt people thought I was just one of those women cutting out gluten. I've found that increasingly people will serve me normal pasta with gluten and expect me to be fine with it, thinking I am a fair-weather gluten hater, not someone who ends up doubled over in pain when I have so much as a sniff of gluten in my meal. Restaurants and dinner parties suddenly became danger zones for me.'

People who cut out gluten by choice take a lot of flak for making life harder for celiacs, just as flexitarians do for making it harder for vegans. But surely the issue here is that, whether you are cutting out gluten for medical reasons or just by preference, whether you are totally plant-based or just trying to avoid meat, you still have every right to be respected in your nutritional requirements. It's entirely unreasonable for someone else to make a judgement about whether your gluten intolerance is legitimate or not. Rather than blaming those who adopt dietary requirements willy-nilly, we should have the courage of our convictions. You have every right to decide what you do and do not eat, so don't bother spending time with people who refuse to respect that.

How to complain

The key to complaining is to do it in a polite, measured and respectful way, to ask the waiting staff for a quiet word and explain (ideally with a smile, and never with a raised voice) what the problem is and how you'd like it to be resolved. Liza, twenty-six, says:

> As a waiter, I never resented customers for complaining. They were generally right. I'm not dumb, I worked in and out of the kitchen and I could tell that our food wasn't always great. Honestly, as long as the customer was polite to me, I never felt any kind of animosity towards them about a food complaint. After all – it's not like I cooked it myself.
>
> I never feel annoyed if someone politely requests a change to their meal either. Sometimes it's annoying to have to go back to the kitchen because our chefs might shout at us, but that's not the customer's fault.
>
> Also, it makes life a lot easier if they say what they want. Your options are usually either a replacement for the food, a different dish from the menu or to just have it taken off the bill. As long as you haven't eaten the whole thing, then everywhere I've worked has been happy to do any of those things, but it's quicker and easier if you explain from the outset which one you'd like it to be.

Complaining doesn't mean that you subsequently skip leaving a tip. In most restaurants (though there are exceptions) the tip is for the waiting staff, not the chef, so if it's the food that you're complaining about, skipping the tip just means that the waiting staff who dealt with your complaint have been penalised, which is not fair. It's more appropriate to complain about the food but still leave a full tip.

If the service has been really terrible you might consider not tipping, but again it depends on whether the waiting staff are understaffed and doing their best, or if they're snooty, judgemental people who can't be bothered to take your order. If it's the former, consider being the bigger person and leaving a tip. If it's the latter, it's up to you.

When I go to a restaurant or hotel where the staff are run off their feet and clearly not working with a big enough team, I will often email the management afterwards to say that I had a great time and the staff were doing their best, but that they were clearly short-handed and that they should consider hiring some extra team members. I'm sure that these emails are often ignored, but occasionally I get a reply saying that they've hired more people. Even if it achieves nothing, it means I've taken an active step to let the establishment know that they're not treating their staff fairly, and, sadly, a business is often more likely to listen to a customer than to a team member.

Complaining has changed a lot since the invention of the Internet. Where once upon a time we were obliged to tell people to their faces that their food was shit or their hotel was uncomfortable, now we can smile at the people in real life and send a snarky tweet. I'm not sure it has really brought out the best in anyone. The key factor in making a complaint is the human interaction. You can sense whether or not the other person is remorseful for the experience, and you can explain to them directly why you're upset.

If you look at the tweets sent to rail companies, hotels, supermarkets and restaurants you'll see streams of abuse. People who are probably perfectly mild-mannered in real life turn into complete monsters when they complain online, saying things like 'I am disgusted' about a slightly late train, or 'You deserve to lose your jobs' over stale sandwiches.

It's almost as if years of not complaining in real life have created a social-media pressure cooker which reduces complaints to their strongest possible form – as if we feel freed by the ability to complain without having to hear another human voice and so we do it in the angriest, nastiest possible way.

This is the wrong kind of rude. If you can't stand by your rudeness in person, then there is probably something off about it. We're in the business of condoning the kind of rude which calmly asserts consumer rights and requests a timely replacement. Not the kind of rude created by social media, which tells Karen in Customer Services to go fuck herself because the jar of salsa you've purchased is two days past its sell-by date.

Businesses have teams dedicated to dealing with complaints over social media; however any complaint you make will almost certainly be met by a request for you to send your payment details privately – whether you're on Facebook, Twitter or Instagram – so it would be more sensible to message them directly rather than go down the public shaming route. It's easy to forget that everyone can see your tweets – even those in the conversation. If you kick off about a cold sausage roll and call the staff working in your local Greggs selfish twats, then it might end up saying more about you than it does about everyone's favourite bakery.

During a journey between Edinburgh and London, when my seat reservation had been cancelled, I entered into a long row with a social-media staff member for Virgin Trains, painstakingly detailing every aspect of my sub-par journey. Funnily enough, there was nothing he could do from 100 miles away in an office. In the end, I decided to take my frustration offline, dragged my bag and my husband to the first-class compartment, sat down and, when asked whether I had a first-class ticket, explained what had happened and asked whether he was really going to make me sit in the luggage rack for another six hours, or whether he was going to declassify. To my relief, he went for the latter option.

It didn't matter how many furious tweets I sent from my Twitter account, nor did it matter that I had 18,000 followers and a verified blue tick; the only way I was getting a seat was by making a polite face-to-face complaint. Complaining properly is assertive and respectable. Slinging abuse at strangers on the Internet – no matter how angry you are – is not the right kind of rude.

The right kind of rude: as a consumer

- Do not click at waiting staff. Do not sleep with people who click at waiting staff. Do not be friends with people who click at waiting staff.

- There is nothing wrong with making a complaint as long as it is done politely.

- You have every right to expect services to be carried out with the appropriate 'care and skill', as the Consumer Rights Act states.

- Complaining in person will usually get you a quicker result than making a complaint online.

- When you complain you should also state how you want the issue to be fixed, rather than make the member of staff play a guessing game.

- When it comes to allergies you should be as rude as you need to be. Is it really worth playing fast and loose with your health?

- Anyone who makes you feel like a bad person for making a polite complaint has their own issues to deal with.
- Members of staff will not think that you're a horrible person for making a polite complaint.
- After you've complained it's still better to leave a tip, unless the waiter has been actively rude to you. If you're nervous about complaining, remember that you are going to tip and that will prevent you from seeming like a bad person.
- Complaining can be done with a smile, and should never, ever be done with a raised voice. If you lose your temper, you lose the argument.
- Try to remember that the business you're buying a service from isn't doing you a favour, so complaining isn't being ungrateful.

Rosa Parks

Rosa Louise McCauley Parks (1913–2005) was an American activist in the civil rights movement. She is often described as 'the First Lady of civil rights'.

Parks was born in Alabama and grew up just outside Montgomery. In 1932 she married Raymond Parks, who was a member of the National Association for the Advancement of Colored People (NAACP). A year later she went back to finish her high-school education, having dropped out aged eleven to take care of her mother and grandmother. In 1943 she became the secretary of the Montgomery chapter of the NAACP, writing in her autobiography, 'I was the only woman there, and they needed a secretary, and I was too timid to say no.'

Parks's activism didn't start or end with the bus boycott

described below. In 1944, before the boycott, in her capacity as secretary of the Montgomery NAACP, she investigated the gang-rape of Recy Taylor, a black woman from Abbeville, Alabama. She helped to organise the Committee for Equal Justice for Mrs Taylor, which the *Chicago Defender* later described as 'the strongest campaign for equal justice to be seen in a decade'.

The landscape of segregation in Alabama was brutal and entrenched in every aspect of public life. In 1900, Montgomery had passed what is called a 'city ordinance' to segregate bus passengers by race. Conductors were empowered to assign seats to achieve that goal. According to actual legislation, no passenger was required to move or give up their seat and stand if the bus was crowded and no other seats were available, but, perhaps predictably, over time Montgomery bus drivers started requiring black passengers to move when there were no white-only seats left.

According to David J. Garrow:

The first four rows of seats on each Montgomery bus were reserved for whites. Buses had 'colored' sections for black people generally in the rear of the bus, although blacks composed more than 75 per cent of the ridership. The sections were not fixed but were determined by placement of a movable sign. Black people could sit in the middle rows until the white section filled; if more whites needed seats, blacks were to move to seats in the rear, stand, or, if there was no room, leave the bus. Black people could not sit across the aisle in the same row as white people. The driver could move the 'colored' section sign or remove it altogether. If white people were already sitting in the front, black people had to board at the front to pay the fare, then disembark and re-enter through the rear door.

After finishing at work for the day, Parks boarded the Cleveland Avenue bus at around 6 p.m. on Thursday, 1 December 1955 in downtown Montgomery. She paid her fare and sat in an empty seat in the first row of back seats reserved in the so-called 'colored' section. The bus then reached a stop where several white passengers boarded. The driver noted that two or three white passengers were standing, as the front of the bus had filled to capacity, so he moved the 'colored' section sign behind Parks and demanded that four black people give up their seats so that the white passengers could sit.

In Parks's account, 'The driver wanted us to stand up, the four of us. We didn't move at the beginning, but he says, "Let me have these seats." And the other three people moved, but I didn't. The black man sitting next to me gave up his seat.'

Parks moved towards the window seat but did not get up to move to the re-designated 'colored' section. The driver then asked Parks, 'Why don't you stand up?', to which Parks responded, 'I don't think I should have to stand up.' The driver then called the police to arrest her.

When recalling the incident, Parks said: 'When he saw me still sitting, he asked if I was going to stand up, and I said, "No, I'm not." And he said, "Well, if you don't stand up, I'm going to have to call the police and have you arrested." I said, "You may do that."'

Describing the incident in her autobiography, Parks wrote: 'People always say that I didn't give up my seat because I was tired, but that isn't true. I was not tired physically, or no more tired than I usually was at the end of a working day. I was not old, although some people have an image of me as being old then. I was forty-two. No, the only tired I was, was tired of giving in.'

After her arrest Parks became an icon of the civil rights movement, but the fairy-tale version of her story often skips out a few major factors, such as the fact that, due to economic sanctions used against activists, she lost her job at the department store where she worked. Or that her husband had to leave his job after his boss forbade him to discuss his wife or her legal case. Still, Parks continued her work and by the time she died, aged ninety-two, she was one of the most famous activists in the world.

Of course Parks's refusal to give up her seat wasn't 'rude'; it was right. Unquestionably, undeniably, unarguably right. But in the eyes of the people around her – the people who believed that white people deserved better treatment and special privileges – she was being extremely 'rude'. And sometimes that's the thing about being rude: you have to act with integrity and allow yourself to believe that your judgement is correct; if you don't feel you're wrong, then you shouldn't allow anyone else to convince you that you are.

Most of us will never do anything as brave as Rosa Parks did, and most of us won't make a fraction of the difference to the world around us that she did, but the point is still there. Rosa Parks held her ground because she knew that what she was doing was right; she didn't let manners or (extremely racist) social conventions prevent her from this incredible show of strength. We should all try to emulate that, whatever the scale.

Surely the sentiment that she describes, being tired of giving in, is one that women all over the world can relate to; but unless we start to do something about it we're going to be tired for the rest of our lives.

CHAPTER SEVEN

RUDE AT WORK

Most of us had a shit first job. It's a rite of passage. Mine was one of my earliest experiences of how badly wrong things can go if you're afraid to be rude.

My job was simple – I worked behind the till of my local village shop, which sold everything from sweets to sponges, between 2 p.m. and 5 p.m. on Saturdays. Everything went fine until my second shift, when my co-worker told me that we were entitled to one free drink per shift – quite a generous offering when you're making £3 an hour. Following her lead, I drank a Diet Coke and then, unsurprisingly, I needed to pee. But I didn't want to be rude.

Peeing, despite the fact that all of us do it, had wiggled its way into my brain as something to be ashamed of. Something not to talk about. Something rude. I didn't know where the bathroom was and I was too embarrassed by the rudeness of the question to ask. So I made my way through a very uncomfortable few hours and the second I finished I legged it towards home. Unfortunately, the twenty-minute walk was more than my bladder could handle, and so I found myself having a pee in a bush by the side of the road. Not a dignified or a comfortable experience, I can promise you.

You'd have thought that the indignity of peeing in a bush would have been enough to hammer the message home: better to be rude than to suffer. But, of course, it didn't. It took more than ten years for me to learn that, when it comes to the workplace, being rude gets you places you want to go, prevents you from being pushed around and, yes, helps you to avoid situations like peeing in a bush. In those ten years I let a boss refer to me as 'whatshername' or occasionally 'whatshername with the tits', permitted other people to take credit for my ideas, held my tongue in meetings, stayed late for no money or advantage, allowed my clothing to be critiqued, never asked for more money or seniority – the list goes on and on. And while, for a long time, I assumed that I was the only one letting herself be fucked over, it turns out that in fact it is happening to women all over the world.

Name games

When I worked at the PR company in central London, my job was to answer the phone, organise catering for meetings, clear up and set up meeting rooms and look after the office diary. What followed was six months of smiling politely while people in suits left meeting rooms with chewing gum in their coffee cups, used tissues on the tables, banana skins on chairs and biscuit wrappers thrown on the floor. Not once did it occur to me to ask the people with whom I worked day in, day out to throw their own used tissues in the bin.

In my tenure as a receptionist I also let people call me Becky every day because I was scared to correct them, and when your name has more than two syllables people seem unable to resist shortening it. My name is Rebecca, or very occasionally Bex. I don't want people to call me Becky because it's not my name.

Correcting someone who gets your name wrong should be

about the easiest thing a person can do. 'Oh, it's not Charlie, it's Charles' – six words and you've avoided the problem. But when you've been raised in the expectation that you will prioritise other people's feelings above your own, as so many women have been, and you're aware of the mortification that saying someone's name wrong can cause, it's hard to form the words 'That's not my name.'

Nathalie, an architect, said:

> I worked in an office for six years. When I was very junior someone called me Nattie, and it stuck. I was called Nattie every single day, didn't matter who was talking to me – even the intern who was fifteen years younger than me, they all called me Nattie. To start with I felt too junior to say anything, like it would be precocious or disrespectful. Then after a while, when I'd been promoted, I felt too insecure to say anything, like it would make people think I was up myself and flaunting my promotion if I asked to be called by my full name. Eventually I left, and when I started my new job I swore that I wouldn't let them call me anything other than Nathalie.
>
> On my first day someone asked if I went by Nat and I took a deep breath and said, 'Not really, no.' They called me Nat anyway and I couldn't bring myself to be rude and say, 'No, really, it's Nathalie.' It was a new job at a new firm, and I needed people to like me. Telling my co-worker to use my full name felt like a rude thing to do, so I didn't. I've been there three years and people still call me Nat.

No doubt some would argue that being called by a diminutive that you didn't choose is no big deal. But it's called a diminutive for a reason – it literally diminishes your name. Makes it smaller. In a world where women struggle to achieve equal pay, something as small as being called by the unshortened, more adult and more assertive version of your name can make a difference.

Who are you more nervous to go into a meeting with, Rosie or Rosemary? Angelica or Jelly? Suzanna or Suze? Shortened nicknames are often what parents use to make their children's names sound more fitting for a baby – not something you want done to you in the workplace (unless it's at your own request). It might seem like a friendly gesture, but using a nickname for someone without their consent undermines them, and, while it might well be an an innocent mistake, there might be a darker side to it.

Either way, if you ditch the fear of being rude you can cheerfully correct whoever is calling you Liz rather than Elizabeth until they stop doing it. That's the thing with fear of rudeness, it actively puts someone else's comfort (not being told off for using the wrong name) above your own benefit (sounding like the most impressive version of yourself). This kind of timid behaviour in the workplace is common even in the most impressive and high-powered women.

Apologies

You will be totally unsurprised to read that women apologise more than men. Studies have shown this time and time again. The reason, according to an article published in *Psychological Science* in 2010, is that 'women have a lower threshold for what constitutes offensive behaviour' and therefore are more likely to see a need to say sorry. You can say that again.

At the time of writing it's 2.45 in the afternoon and I have already apologised for opening the door to my apartment building while someone was standing quite near it, trying to get on a Tube, wanting a lid for my coffee, the fact that someone else on my team hadn't done a piece of work they were supposed to do, and for using the microwave in the kitchen when another person came in looking to use it. And that's me trying not to apologise too much.

The introduction of the power of rude into your daily life, particularly your work life, is often tricky to navigate, as a change in behaviour of any description often confuses those around you. Banning the word 'sorry' from your life is a great aim, but trust me, it's nigh on impossible to do. However, one really easy trick that you can start using straight away is to reframe the way in which you apologise.

Saying you're sorry when you've actually done something wrong is great, it's a sign of strength to be able to acknowledge your own failings. However, there is a tendency for women to use 'sorry' as a catch-all, often when what they really mean is 'thank you'. If you can swap out those sorries you can assert yourself as a more competent person. Rather than 'I'm sorry for keeping you waiting,' try, 'Thank you so much for your patience.' Instead of 'I'm sorry for not understanding,' go with 'Thank you for taking the time to explain.' In doing so you're still acknowledging the favour done you by the other person, but not by suggesting that you yourself are in the wrong. The person you thank feels that their efforts have been appreciated, but you haven't admitted any unnecessary fault.

Emails

An example of how scared we are to be rude is the way that we email. It's a well-observed phenomenon that women litter their emails with self-deprecating language. The worst offenders are qualifying words like 'just' and 'quick', statements such as 'I'm no expert' and timid, questioning language such as 'Is there any chance?'

In an article published on LinkedIn, Ellen Petry Lease, who worked at Google, describes an informal experiment she led after she noticed that the women she worked with were constantly using the word 'just' as a qualifier about their work ('I just wanted to ask,' 'I'm just going to edit that document,' 'I'm just wondering'). Lease writes:

> In a room full of young entrepreneurs, a nice even mix of men and women, I asked two people – a guy and a girl – each to spend three minutes speaking about their start-ups. I asked them to leave the room to prepare, and while they were gone I asked the audience secretly to tally the number of times they each said the word 'just'. Sarah went first. Pens moved pretty briskly in the audience's hands. Some tallied five, some six. When Paul spoke, the pen moved . . . once. Even the speakers were blown away when we revealed that count.

A 2006 study by Carol Waseleski titled 'Gender and the Use of Exclamation Points in Computer-Mediated Communication' found that women were more likely to use exclamation marks as softeners in their emails. Why? Because it makes you sound perky and enthusiastic rather than direct and confrontational. 'Thanks for this!' reads as lighter and less serious than 'Thanks for this.' Women, the research concludes, are considerably more worried about how their written communication comes across. As one viral tweet said, 'Behind every great woman are four other women who proofread her email for her real quick when they had a second.'

Back in 2017, a man named Martin Schnieder accidentally used his female co-worker's email signature and noticed an immediate difference in the way he was treated by his correspondents. He continued doing so for the rest of the week out of interest and was shocked by the experience, writing on Twitter: 'I was in hell. Everything I asked or suggested was questioned. Clients I could [usually handle] in my sleep were condescending. One asked if I was single.'

In response to this discrepancy between how men and women email, plug-ins have been developed which highlight or underline every time you use qualifying words such as 'just', 'quick', 'sorry' and 'I think'. The idea is that at the end of writing an email you look back at the number of qualifying phrases and self-deprecating expressions you've used and delete them, so that you can email 'like a man'. Unfortunately, installing a plug-in so that your emails read as more confident and masculine (ruder, if you will) is not a catch-all. In 2017 the journalist Amelia Tait detailed numerous case studies of women who email 'like men' being regarded as aggressive or cold when they dropped the nice-lady language. She writes in the *Spectator*: 'Can women win? Without exclamations, they might seem rude – with them, they may seem unprofessional.'

Of course, you shouldn't have to worry about any of this. It should be entirely possible for you to show up at work, do your job and go home, without anyone making a judgement about you based on the tone of your email or how smiley you are in the lift. Sadly, that isn't the case. The world of work is not always kind to women – especially not rude women. In fact, there is an entire section of language devoted to smacking them back into their place – words which are only ever used to describe women who eschew hyper-feminine politeness:

- ball-breaker
- ballsy

- bitchy
- bridezilla
- catty
- diva
- feisty
- high-maintenance
- hormonal
- hysterical
- pushy
- shrill
- stroppy

With an entire lexicon of loaded language designed to convey the message that a woman is misbehaving through her rudeness, is there really any wonder that we email with chirpy exclamation marks and end our missives by claiming that we 'really hope that you're well'?

And so the vicious circle goes on. We email like Office Barbie for fear of being seen as rude, and so it becomes expected that we will do so, and women who skip the smiley-face emojis and don't 'hope that you're enjoying this lovely weather!' are written off as ball-breaking bitches.

There is no easy solution and no magic wand to change the way in which women are perceived in the workplace, or indeed in the world. Using the power of rude does sometimes mean that you are going to be perceived as a 'ball-breaker', frustrating as that might be.

Hepeating

If you work in an office, you may well be familiar with the sin of 'hepeating', a word coined in 2017 and popularised by Professor Nicole Gugliucci, who explained it in a Twitter thread thus: 'My friends coined a word: hepeated. For when a woman suggests an idea and it's ignored, but then a guy says same thing and everyone loves it.' Classic signs of hepeating are when men start sentences with 'Just coming off the back of what [your name] said,' or 'To build on what [your name] said,'.

It's possible to dismiss hepeating as no big deal or a low-level workplace irritation, like when someone uses your favourite mug; but the problem is, hepeating can actually erode your career progress if the rest of the people in the meeting remember the idea coming from the hepeater rather than you. Esther says:

> I had a guy in my seminar group at university who would never read the book. Fair enough, that was his choice. But instead of just sitting quietly and letting us discuss the book, he would hepeat whatever we said. And the tutor just lapped it up, thinking this bloke was some kind of genius, when actually he was just taking the best part of what we said and slightly rephrasing it. Admittedly, a lot of the problem was this tutor, who for some reason chose to ignore his copycat behaviour, but this guy got top marks, was always paired with the best people in the class for group work, and generally coasted through without doing any work.
>
> Towards the end of the module I got really sick of it, so whenever he hepeated me I would just look him straight in the eye and repeat what I had said again. We'd go back and forth

until the tutor stopped us. He was too ballsy to be upset by it, and he kept doing it to other people, but he stopped ripping my points off and I felt like on some level I had won.

Tackling hepeating at work is harder than in a university environment because we're all supposed to be acting like functional adults, and unfortunately, as we know from the previous research in this chapter, women have to be beyond reproach in professional settings to avoid being labelled as bitches. So occasional instances of hepeating might have to be ignored, but if you've got a regular hepeater, there's nothing wrong with an icy smile and the words, 'Yes, which is what I was saying.'

Back in 2017, CNBC asked Harvard public policy professor and behavioural economist Iris Bohnet, the author of *What Works: Gender Equality by Design*, 'What should you do if you are being hepeated?' Bohnet suggested that the best way to combat hepeating at work is to invest in a kind of 'micro-sponsorship', which means enlisting a few co-workers to advocate for you when you've been wronged. Bohnet explains: 'Become vigilant about attributing comments to the people who made them first. Everyone, men and women, can become a micro-sponsor. Sadly, the gender of the observers only plays a small role. We all tend to associate authority and expertise with men and thus are more likely to listen to men than women,' she says. 'And of course, these stereotypes are constantly reinforced.'

So rather than saying, 'Actually I was talking,' or 'You just ripped off my idea,' you say: 'I think [colleague's name] was talking,' or 'Yes, I think that's what [colleague's name] was saying before.' By interceding for others you are not perceived to be out for yourself or self-promoting (both of which are totally fine, but stigmatised inside and outside the workplace), and in theory you build a network wherein other people will provide the same service in return, pointing out the hepeating without getting you labelled as moody or difficult.

The skill here is to be assertive (rude, if you like) without being perceived as a bitch, because while it's your prerogative to be a bitch, if people in your workplace write you off as such then your life will be harder, the whole endeavour will have failed you and I'll owe you a refund for this book.

Should we need to go to these lengths to stop men from ripping off our ideas and presenting them as their own? Of course we shouldn't. But the idea here is to harness the power of rude to make your life easier, which, unfortunately, means dealing in realities rather than ideals.

Salary

No one likes asking for a raise, and the perception is that women like it less than men. The idea that women 'aren't good' at it is often mooted as a major cause of the gender pay gap. But this is technically untrue – women do ask for pay rises; however, research suggests that their methods are often unsuccessful. We'll cover the agony of rudeness and money more fully in the money chapter, but it would be remiss to talk about office-based rudeness without looking at the stress of asking for a raise.

For women who are afraid of being perceived as rude, asking for a raise is about as painful as it gets. You're being expected to approach someone who has given you a job, tolerated your work, paid you a salary and announce that none of it is good enough. Asking for a raise feels spoiled, entitled and ungrateful. Of course, it isn't any of those things, and if you don't ask for at least a small raise year on year, then with inflation you can end up earning less than you did when you started at the company. But rudephobia is not bound by logic, it's born of a visceral nausea which arises whenever we contemplate doing something which might make people think we are rude.

As a journalist with several years of experience, I had been working for the same publication for nearly two years before I realised that I was being paid less than other people, and that my daily rate was almost half what the NUJ recommended a journalist should be paid. So, after two weeks of worrying about it, I requested permission from my manager to ask for a raise, and when that permission came I then sent an email saying:

> Dear [redacted], I'm so sorry to ask, but I was wondering if there was any chance that we might be able to discuss my day rate? I feel that I'm a valuable member of the team, my traffic is strong and I have been part of the organisation for almost two years. I completely understand if not, but I would be keen to discuss it with you.

Straight out of the 'emailing like a woman' playbook, I apologised for even suggesting we might talk about a raise. In the end, after asking the same profusely apologetic question several times, I was offered a small salary increase. It was still considerably less than the union-recommended day rate, but I was so shocked by my own boldness that it didn't occur to me for a second that I might attempt to negotiate.

Much of the writing about women and the pay gap foists the responsibility on to women, telling them that it's their own fault for not asking. But, just as emailing like a man can portray a woman as aggressive, asking for a raise can result in the same thing. Sara Laschever, co-author of the book *Why Women Don't Ask*, says that women who are assertive with regard to issues like their salary are often perceived as aggressive and are sometimes punished for it. 'They tend to get rebuffed, and socially ostracized. Other women see this and realize it looks scary and risky to behave like them. Far better, they think, to sit tight and wait to be offered whatever it is – a promotion, pay rise, good project – rather than ask for it.'

But, of course, this is no way to further your career. In full accordance with Sara Laschever's theory is a story from Millie, a twenty-seven-year-old creative:

> I worked as an unpaid intern for several months after I graduated from art school. Eventually I was told that I was going to be offered a paid role and I was over the moon. Then I looked at the offer: it was less than the minimum wage, with almost no holiday and no benefits. So I spent a whole day psyching myself up and then went to ask to renegotiate. My boss told me that he was hurt beyond belief that I could be so unkind to him. He told me that he was paying me out of his business and by asking for more I had insulted him. I couldn't live on what he was offering so I had to leave. For years afterwards I was scared of asking for a raise because I thought it would mean that my boss started crying and telling me how rude and ungrateful I was.

Something of a Catch-22 situation, right? We don't ask for raises so the pay gap is our own fault, but when we do ask for them we're arrogant bitches who need to be reminded of our place. Or we're spoiled and ungrateful brats who don't really care about the work. You'd be forgiven for looking at that dilemma and deciding that there is no good answer.

But there is an answer, and you can probably guess what

it is: rudeness. Learning to disregard other people's comfort with your 'arrogance' and firmly requesting to be paid what you are worth. Because if enough women do it, we can shift the paradigm. It's also important to try to encourage the other women in your work life to adopt this kind of behaviour, so that you're not the big, bossy one who constantly asks for unreasonable things like a pay rise and better working conditions.

Talk to your colleagues about asking for more money. Discuss whether you've had a raise, or whether you've asked for one and then been rebuffed. Employers hate it when their employees have transparent conversations about money with each other – for a good reason. A workforce of people who are having an ongoing discussion about salary are far more likely to ask for pay rises and get them. The best way to negate the sexist and unfair perception that asking for a raise means women don't love their job enough is to use the old-fashioned 'I am Spartacus' rule. If everyone is asking for pay reviews, no one woman can be sacrificed on the altar of 'She doesn't really seem to love her job.'

Bossy

The problems with the word 'bossy' are well documented, but here's a quick refresher course: it's a word, almost never applied to men, which you often hear used to describe little girls who like to organise or exhibit leadership skills. It's a way of framing those skills in a negative light when they apply to someone female, and as such the word should be avoided. However, despite the fact that you can buy T-shirts which read 'I'm not bossy, I'm the boss,' the damage has already been done and there are plenty of women all over the world who feel uncomfortable being in charge.

There are plenty of good reasons to fear being the boss. Shelley Zalis, CEO of the Female Quotient, wrote for *Forbes* magazine: 'An analysis of news coverage of CEOs by the Rockefeller Foundation found not only that the media covered the personal lives of female CEOs more frequently than male CEOs, but that 80 per cent of news stories pegged the blame for failed company turnarounds to CEOs when they were women, compared to just 31 per cent when they were men.'

But beyond the glass cliff (when a woman is brought into a failing company to improve the diversity optics and is then blamed for being unable to save an unsalvageable business), there is also a sense of discomfort in being the boss which stems from internalised misogyny. Internalised misogyny is when women absorb the sexist messages that they are bombarded with. For instance, if you accidentally assume that a doctor is a man and a nurse is a woman, that's internalised misogyny. It's not that you're a bad person or a rubbish feminist, it's just that these things get ingrained into our subconscious and they're hard to shake. There will always be a tiny part of me which hears the word 'boss' and sees Don Draper drinking a glass of Scotch in a glass corner office. And while neither you nor I need to feel guilty about that tendency, it rears its ugly head when we are offered leadership roles.

Guilt

Nola, thirty-one, works in finance. She's always been a high-flyer (though she would be embarrassed to hear me say that about her). She got a top degree, joined a graduate scheme, worked her way up and now has a senior role where she is about a decade younger than everyone else at her level. During the hiring process for her job, the CEO came to her and requested that she apply to replace her boss. She was uneasy about doing it, citing her already strained work-life balance. But he assured her that it wouldn't be that much more work because she would be able to delegate to her team.

When Nola was offered the job, we sat in my garden drinking wine and she told me that she felt guilty. 'The other guy who applied is in his mid-forties,' she told me. 'He's got kids and a mortgage. He needs the money more than I do, and if he doesn't get promoted soon then he'll probably miss out.'

I resisted the temptation to chuck the glass of wine at Nola. I and everyone else around the table drowned out her concerns with scorn, telling her that she had to take the role and that she deserved it. When she tried to turn the job down the bosses offered her a retainer bonus, giving her thousands of pounds a year just to stop her from jumping ship. The entire situation seemed perfect. More money, her own office, a bigger team. The dream.

Nola is a genius at her job. Unfortunately, when we all shoved her towards taking the enormous promotion, we forgot to think about what it might cost her. The next time I saw her she was clearly exhausted and two hours late to meet for drinks. It was 9 p.m. and the earliest she had left work for weeks. When pressed, she told me that she was doing her own workload and then staying hours and hours after close of play to redo the work done by team members, or finish things they hadn't had time to do. She was doing the work of her deputy – the man who had applied for her job – as well as all of her own load, because she couldn't bring herself to confront the man she'd beaten for the role. 'It was so embarrassing for him that I got the job,' she told me, 'I didn't want to add to that by telling him off. He knows I won't say anything to him, so he just does whatever he wants.'

We had convinced Nola to take this enormous, impressive, important job without stopping to question what it might do to her – one of the most conflict-adverse people I have ever met in my life. She couldn't find the voice to tell the people on her team, especially the man who believed he should have her job, that they needed to get things done, so instead she was working herself into the ground to try to fill in the gaps.

This isn't a neat anecdote, because she's a real person and this is her real life. At the time of writing she's still pulling an eighty-hour week, sleeping five hours a night and views her marathon training as 'a rest'. She is, she claims, trying to be better about telling her team that they need to do their own work. But unfortunately, once you instigate a culture in which anything that doesn't get done by you will be picked up by your boss, it's hard to undo it.

Orson Welles apparently used to hire someone especially so he could then fire them on the first day of a production, thus demonstrating that he was a tough guy who meant business; and while that's obviously a bit on the extreme side (and actually a storyline in an episode of *Friends*), you can see where he was coming from. If Nola had walked into the job and stamped her authority all over the place, she wouldn't still be in a situation where she writes reports for people who should in theory be getting her coffee. That said, we know that getting it 'right', aka being a boss who is an actual boss, doesn't always work out for women in the same way that it does for men.

The right kind of rude: at work

- Correct someone the day they get your name wrong, not a week later.

- Keep written records, so if anyone suggests that your tone was aggressive or harsh you'll be able to demonstrate otherwise.

- Ask about pay grades, and encourage clarity surrounding how much everyone is earning. If you find out that you're being paid less, don't give a second thought to asking for a raise.

- Asking for more money might feel stressful and scary, but remember, unless you work for a very small business, a raise of £2,000 (which would make a tangible difference to your life) will make very little difference to their bottom line.

- You're not being a brat for wanting to be paid for your work. Whether a friend asks you to help out with a 'project' or a company wants to offer you 'exposure' or 'experience', that's modern slavery and it's not right.

- Burn-out is a real thing: if your company is working you too hard or setting unrealistic deadlines, you should tell them – without feeling guilty or ashamed.

- It is never ungrateful or unreasonable to turn down work.

- Calling people out for sexist behaviour doesn't have to make you a killjoy. You can do it with a smile. Top tip – if someone is telling sexist jokes in your office, pretend you don't get the joke and ask them to explain it. Continue not to understand until they've dug themselves into a nice big hole.

- Taking a sick day is not a big deal, and it's a lot better than bringing a contagious illness into the office.

- Just because someone is senior to you does not give them the right to treat you with anything other than respect.

Anna Wintour

Anna Wintour was born in 1949 and has been editor-in-chief of American *Vogue* since 1988. She's the longest-serving editor of any *Vogue* and famously runs the magazine with an iron rod. She has been followed around by accusations of meanness throughout her career. During her tenure at British *Vogue* people called her 'Nuclear Wintour', and later at American *Vogue* her underlings referred to her as the 'Wintour of Discontent'.

It's well known that the character of Miranda Priestly in *The Devil Wears Prada* is based on Wintour – the book was written by Lauren Weisberger, Wintour's erstwhile assistant, who immortalised her right down to the detail that Wintour allegedly won't allow anyone else to share the same lift as her in the office.

A friend of hers told the *Observer*: 'I think she has been very rude to a lot of people in the past, on her way up – very terse. She doesn't do small talk. She is never going to be friends with her assistant.' Another friend told the *Guardian*, 'At some stage in her career, Anna Wintour stopped being Anna Wintour and became "Anna Wintour", at which point, like wings of a stately home, she closed off large sections of her personality to the public.' 'I think she enjoys not being completely approachable. Just her office is very intimidating. You have to walk about a mile into the office before you get to her desk and I'm sure it's intentional,' said long-term colleague Grace Coddington. 'I don't find her to be accessible to people she doesn't need to be accessible to,' agrees *Vogue* publisher Tom Florio.

Do men often worry about being accessible when they're at the top of an enormous company? I don't think so. Unlike a lot of powerful women, Anna Wintour doesn't feel the need to make herself seem sweet, fluffy and available. She's the editor of one of the most famous publications in the world. She's a powerful, busy, influential woman. And she doesn't waste time on trying to come across as 'nice'.

Commenting on her reputation, Wintour said: 'I read that I'm an ice queen, I'm the Sun King, I'm an alien fleeing from District 9 and I'm a dominatrix, so I reckon that makes me lukewarm royalty with a whip from outer space.' Not the words of a woman who is losing sleep over her public perception, then.

Perhaps the secret to Wintour's spectacular success is that she has used the time that some women spend trying to augment their reputation so that they come across as lovely. While the stories about her are admittedly fearsome, and I don't suggest for a moment that we normal people start insisting on our own lifts, her success is undeniable. Wintour has edited *Vogue* since the 1980s, despite the fact that publishing was a famously male-dominated industry, and she's been able to keep a print magazine thriving during a time when circulation figures of magazines seem to get lower and lower. She is a testament to what we can achieve if we worry less about how people regard us, and more about doing an extraordinarily good job.

There aren't enough hours in the day to be at the top of your game and at the same time worry whether every single person you spoke to today left with the impression that you're a sweet yet funny, playful yet serious, intelligent yet light person. Drop the worry. Accept that, just like the Queen of Mean herself, not everyone is going to like you, and then get on with being so good at your job that no one cares whether you're nice or not. What might *you* achieve if you devoted the time you spend worrying about being likeable, personable, sweet or popular to something productive?

CHAPTER EIGHT

RUDE ABOUT MONEY

When I was eighteen, I finished school and moved to London to be a writer. Only, because it wasn't 1950 and I wasn't a Mitford, in order to be a writer I needed to get a job, so I found a part-time, live-in role as a nanny. The arrangement was pretty decent – I got a room, £100 a week for twenty-five hours of childcare and some of my meals paid for. I was in central London, I had enough money to buy drinks and cigarettes, and when I didn't I had enough charm to get by. I only needed a few hours of sleep a week and occasionally to lick a vegetable and I looked the very picture of health, so I was able to combine nannying with a full-on social life. All in all, it was an extremely sweet deal.

Only once I started working did I realise that it was a rather flexible arrangement. Twenty-five hours during term time, yes. But during the school holidays I would be required nine to five, bringing my weekly total to thirty-five hours and meaning that I was doing a whole lot of childcare on a whole lot of hangovers, and that my 'writing time' (which was very often sleeping time) was gone.

'Are they paying you extra for that?' my friends asked when I explained the situation.

'I don't know,' I answered. 'I didn't ask.'

It wasn't that it didn't occur to me to ask – in fact it was all I could think about. I was burning up with the unfairness of all this unpaid extra work. I'd built myself a routine, spending the mornings wandering the fanciest parts of London, settling into a café to work on the (very bad) novel I was writing, before slotting into Mary Poppins mode at 2.30 p.m.

My boyfriend at the time found this entire thing impossible to comprehend. 'Just tell them you want £5 an hour for each extra hour,' he told me, as if it was the easiest thing in the world. Twice I tried to have that conversation, and twice I failed. I was an adult, I had the skills required to move to a new city and start a new life, but I could not bring myself to ask what felt like the rudest question in the world: please will you pay me for my time?

Eventually the end of the week came, and I was paid £20 for the extra ten hours – £2 an hour. I'm embarrassed to admit that I said thank you very much and smiled like I'd won the lottery rather than saying, 'That's very kind of you but I think £60 would be more appropriate.' With retrospect it's easy to think that I should have negotiated an appropriate higher rate for my work during the school holidays, setting an expectation on both sides of the arrangement. But, of course, I didn't. I didn't want to be rude.

It would be easy to write this off as a youthful lack of confidence, but it's behaviour which continued into my late twenties. When I sold my first novels, I asked my agent to stop negotiating because I didn't want to seem 'ungrateful'. When I was offered my first full-time job working on a women's magazine it literally did not occur to me to ask for more money. My husband, on the other hand, has negotiated a salary hike on every job offer he's ever received. When I asked him why, he told me: 'Because it's easier to ask for more money now rather than further down the line.' He didn't realise I was trying to find out why he felt able to ask at all, assuming I was merely enquiring about the timing.

Talking about money is awkward, uncomfortable, embarrassing. Generally speaking, it's something that we as women work hard to avoid doing. Unfortunately, no good comes of that. And having any money to talk about at all is a privilege and a recent development.

Money is one of the main means by which women have been oppressed over the course of history. Money means power, freedom and independence. Without money you're not going anywhere – which proved convenient for a society that liked women for cooking, sex and child-rearing but not much else.

A history of money

Financial restrictions on women applied all the way across society. Poor women worked, but their income could be claimed by their husbands for any reason at all. Rich women generally didn't inherit, and unless they married would become a burden on their male relatives, living at the family home as spinster aunts dependent on the goodwill of their brothers to bestow allowances.

Women weren't allowed a bank account in their own name until 1975. They also weren't allowed to apply for a loan or credit card without their father's or husband's co-signature until the mid 1970s. Before then most women were given money for 'housekeeping' by their husbands. Ironically, women would be expected to balance a household budget and keep everyone clothed and fed on whatever they were given, but they still weren't considered to be responsible enough for something bonkers like a private bank account or a credit card, let alone a mortgage.

As with so much of the rudeness we talk about in this book,

there is always the question of privilege. Down through history there have been women who inherited money because they had no male siblings (there was no such thing as a British heiress with a brother) and were able to enjoy the freedom the money afforded them. But, for the most part, until the late twentieth century money was controlled by men and considered to be the business of men, leaving women with fewer options and far less power. I'm sad to say that, while we've come a long way from the obligation for your father to allow you a bank account, we're hardly there yet. We still have a gender pay gap.

The pay gap

The pay gap is a hotly debated and much-misunderstood concept. Many people think it means men being paid more than women for doing the same job. In theory, this is illegal and already a protected characteristic. In practice, it does happen – not because employers seek out women to hire and pay them less per hour than men, but because men are more likely to ask for pay rises and then be given them.

In companies where bonuses are used as incentives, the pay gap is also caused by the values placed on the ways in which men and women traditionally work. Many bonus structures tend to favour winning new business and having new successes, something which is often associated with male workplace behaviour. Women are more likely to maintain ongoing client relationships, which is less likely to be rewarded with a bonus.

The pay gap is most significant between women of colour who have children, and white men. Men generally make more money after they become fathers, while women almost universally earn less in the years following the birth of a child.

To some extent this is associated with taking time off from the workplace to provide childcare, something which still almost always falls to the mother – in 2019, only 2 per cent of parents used their eligibility for shared parental leave.

In the UK, companies with more than 250 employees are obliged to publish their gender pay gap. On average it was 8.6 per cent for people who are in full-time employment (an important caveat, as pay gap deniers will often argue that the gap is caused by women 'working less').

One popular response to the pay gap statistics is to explain that the pay gap is caused because a small number of men at the very top of a company take home extremely large salaries, which throws off the average. To which the obvious response is: why is it always 'small numbers of men' who are earning these socking great salaries?

Another aspect of the pay gap is the 'second shift', which is when women, who are the primary caregivers in the majority of households, finish work on the dot of 5 p.m. and pick up the kids, go home, cook them dinner, clean the house, put the kids to bed, wash and iron some school uniforms and then finally collapse in a heap, too tired even to drink a G&T. On the other hand, lots of men stay at work later, but then they go straight home, eat the dinner that has been cooked for them and watch a bit of telly. But they worked late. So they, unlike their partners, get paid.

On average men do sixteen unpaid hours of house-based work a week. Women do twenty-six. Women get less money over a lifetime than men do, despite working just as hard. That isn't fair, and the only way to change it is to talk about it. There was a time when talking about sex was shameful and taboo. These days most of us will chat about rimming over cocktails. It's entirely possible to change the way in which we treat a topic and strip away a taboo if we put our minds to it. Much as we have a responsibility to vote in elections because women died for our right to do so, we have an obligation to get a grip on our finances because the women who came before us could only have dreamed of their own bank accounts, pay cheques and credit cards.

Money and friends

Talking about money in a professional setting is bad enough, but doing it with friends is even worse. Just watch a group of people split a bill in a restaurant and you'll see. Even though everyone knows that paying for what you actually ate is fairer, bill-splitting is very common. It doesn't matter if one of you had a side salad and a glass of tap water while someone else washed down the Chateaubriand with a lovely 2011 Malbec, the ease of splitting trumps the fairness of paying for what you had. Possibly because, if you're rich enough not to care, then you won't give it a second thought, and if you're the member of the friendship group who is adding up whether to default on your water bill or say the words, 'Would anyone mind paying for what we had?', then you're probably lacking in the confidence to do so. While there shouldn't be any shame in being the friend in the group who earns the least, there often is.

Few words strike fear into the heart quite as much as 'group birthday meal'. I went to one recently at an incredibly expensive new restaurant in central London. I was feeling pretty broke after a spate of birthdays and wasn't really in the mood to attend. Neither was anyone else I knew who was going, but we slapped on a smile and turned up, having agreed between us that it wouldn't be more than about £40 a head if we ordered sharing plates and didn't eat too much.

We might have been right, if someone hadn't brought a girlfriend along. Said girlfriend picked at other people's food, though didn't order anything herself, and drank four glasses of wine. At the end of the meal it was decided at her end of the table that she wouldn't pay because she 'didn't eat'. All of us, who were already stressed about the bill, gritted our teeth and took out our cards. The bill split between eight rather than nine was noticeably more expensive. Did we say anything? Of course not. We didn't want to be rude. Instead we paid for this stranger's food and drink and seethed silently about it all night. The birthday girl felt guilty, we felt short-changed, and it soured the evening. If we'd been less afraid of being rude, we would politely have pointed out that she'd drunk a bottle of wine and asked her to pay. She probably wouldn't even have minded. The most frustrating part wasn't so much the money as the resentment of her that none of us seemed able to shake off for the rest of the evening.

I'm not the only one who has found herself in situations like this. Sacha, twenty-nine, tells me:

I was appointed as maid of honour for my school friend's wedding, which meant organising the hen do. I hadn't done it before, but I figured it would be fine. I sent round a poll to pick a date, got an RSVP from everyone and then let everyone know that for a weekend in the countryside with meals and alcohol included it would be £200.

Her friends all came back saying that it would be too expensive. I tried to cut costs where I could, but there just wasn't any way of renting a house and feeding everyone for less. I realise now that I should have told the bride that her friends (most of whom

I didn't know) wouldn't pay the money, but they all told me that if I passed that message on the bride would be upset. So, what did I do? I went £600 into my overdraft subsidising the weekend for a load of women I hadn't met before and haven't seen since.

I know it was the weakest possible way to handle the situation and I'm not proud of it, but I couldn't face talking about money, and I felt like I'd be telling the bride that her friends didn't value her enough to spend their money on her hen.

I was saving for a deposit on a house and I had to tell my boyfriend about it several months later. He was furious and couldn't understand why I would do something like that. He pushed me to ask everyone to give me the money back, but I wouldn't even consider it.

Borrowing money

The most uncomfortable aspect of friendship and money arises when we talk about borrowing or lending cash, because, as we all know, lending money to friends is a bad idea. It's also sometimes unavoidable.

Once, at university, I got my card declined trying to buy a six-pack of Diet Coke and some pita bread. I had a week to wait until more cash was due into my account and panic set in. Ashamed of myself, too proud to call my parents and too afraid of seeming rude to ask my friends, I used a pay-day loan site to borrow £50, at nearly 6,000 per cent APR. I was due to pay back around £85 a week later – a ridiculous amount, but manageable. Unfortunately, there was a glitch at their end and the payment wasn't taken, meaning that I was charged a £50 default fee. I then spent £40 on my phone bill trying to speak to the loan company to correct this. All in all, my refusal to swallow my pride and do the sensible (rude) thing cost me £125. I should just have asked a friend.

Since then I've borrowed and lent friends money, following the rule that you should never lend more than you can afford to lose. Lending to mates can work out just fine. But not always. There's a reason for the expression, 'Neither a borrower nor a lender be.'

Sara, now twenty-eight, then twenty-four, lent her boyfriend £2,000 to help him get out of debt. She explains:

> He didn't ask, to be fair. But he was struggling with his debt situation so I offered to pay it off and then he could pay me back slowly. He was enormously grateful and to start with he was making regular payments. But bit by bit they became later, less regular and then when we broke up (not related), they stopped. I knew I should ask him for them, but I'd already broken up with him, and I hated how asking for the money was going to make me look, so I didn't.
>
> Years later I found out that he had a really well-paying job, so I decided to get in touch with him. I spent two days crafting a really thoughtful email to him, explaining that I wanted the money back but that I was willing to wait, take the payments slowly, whatever he needed. He didn't reply.
>
> In the end the whole conversation was bad for my mental health, so I decided to leave the money. But I'm still so angry with my past self for being so afraid to seem like a bitch by demanding that money back.

Caitlin, thirty-one, had a similar experience. She explains:

> I covered a lot of bills and other costs when I moved into a shared house with two of my girlfriends. To start with I was too caught up in the fun of living together to chase for the money,

and then it seemed too late, and kind of mean to ask. When I did eventually get the confidence to ask them, they ignored the message and I wasn't bold enough to ask again. They both still owe me £150 each.

So lending money can go wrong, and demanding money back can be a terrifying thing to do, especially if you haven't yet embraced the idea of being rude. But actually, a money fight is the perfect way to learn how to be rude. It's awkward, painful and requires you to get your claws out. Once you've survived demanding back money that you're rightfully owed, you've earned your rude stripes.

According to the UK government, your options are as follows:

- Mediation, whereby the person who owes you money attends a discussion witnessed by a neutral third party and you both explain your points of view.

- Court action, whereby the person who owes you money is summoned to court. You can file a court complaint online if you're owed less than £100,000.

- Make an official statutory demand for your money.

Try to keep all conversations about the money you're owed written down on message or email, so that you've got a paper trail if you need to take things further. That said, you'll probably find that once you've found the inner strength to call out the person who owes you money and assert yourself, making it clear that you want repayment in full, chances are they'll pay you back.

Money and relationships

Being honest about your finances is difficult with your friends, but it can be even harder in a relationship. At the start of a romance the last thing you want to do is turn down something fun because you can't afford the ticket, or come across as stingy by not offering to split the bill in an expensive restaurant. But if you don't get rude about money early on, then you make a rod for your own back.

When I first met my husband I was an aspiring journalist/ student/office temp. He was ten years my senior and in a professional role with a good salary, so already there was an enormous gap in our finances. He was incredibly generous, but I was determined not to let him pay for everything, and rather than saying, 'Actually do you mind if we have a bottle of wine at home rather than three rounds of drinks at a pub?' I went further and further into my overdraft. When he was eventually made redundant and had to start watching the pennies, I was guilty at how relieved I felt. It was awful for him, but for me the pressure was finally off.

Much of being in a relationship is being honest about your wants, needs and fears, and that does get easier as your relationship develops. But on the other hand, the longer you are with someone, the more tangled your finances get, and that's not necessarily a good thing. Sharing your money with another person might seem practical if you live together or you've got a lot of joint expenses, but it's important to be cautious about how you do that.

Claire, twenty-eight, found that doing this was not a good idea:

About two years into my relationship with my ex-boyfriend, we decided to merge an account and put our finances more together, seeing as we were moving in together.

I'll be honest, I wasn't sure that I wanted to do it, but he said it made more sense, and when I talked about my concerns he thought that I was rejecting him. I was scared to seem selfish or like I was being stingy, so I went ahead and did it. Unfortunately, it turned out that he had some major debt issues. He was working to pay it off, but lots of things were registered to our shared address and because we had a joint account it had a strong adverse effect on my credit rating.

I've always been financially conservative to the point of being boring, so when I saw that my credit score had taken a massive hit I assumed it was a mistake, but then I realised it was because of Chris, and I was horrified. Neither of us knew that there would be any issue with his credit rating affecting mine, and he didn't do it maliciously. But if I'm honest, I struggled to forgive him for it. I wanted to buy a house, something which has been delayed by this experience.

In the end we broke up, and while I told him it had nothing to do with his debt and my credit rating, it did. I was still too angry with him for pushing me into a joint account, and with myself for being too spineless to say no to the whole thing.

Credit ratings

As Claire found out, getting a joint account with the person you're dating might seem like a good idea, but it's important to be clear about your respective credit scores before you do that, as any issue with debt can have an impact on you. According to the Money Advice Service: 'If one of you has a poor credit history, it's not normally a good idea to open a joint account. Just living with someone, or being married to them, will not affect your credit rating, but as soon as you open a joint bank account together you will be "co-scored". Similarly, being listed on the same bill can create a financial association, so if one of you has an adverse credit rating then it might be worth thinking about splitting the bills up so you pay different things, rather than being jointly named.'

Of course, it's tempting to want to tell the person you love that their debt is no big deal and that you still want to go ahead with the joint account, but try to be realistic about what that will mean for you. Do not be afraid to protect yourself above the other person's feelings. Anyone worth dating will understand that you don't want to tank your chances of buying a house to spare someone else's sensibilities.

Debt shouldn't be a source of shame or judgement, but if you're going to take on someone else's credit rating by sharing an account, you want to do so knowingly, not just because you're uncomfortable admitting to them that you don't want to damage your own credit rating. As women we are raised to put other people's feelings before our own, making sure that they feel happy at the expense of our happiness. It's an impractical, pointless tendency which results in stories like Claire's.

Debt

When you're in love with someone, telling them no becomes hard. Not only do you not want to seem rude, you also don't want to crush their dreams. Unfortunately, being able to say no – or, more specifically, 'I can't afford that' – is an essential part of a relationship.

Amy, twenty-eight, ran up £2,000 of debt because she didn't want to stomp on her boyfriend's dreams:

My boyfriend and I were walking around London one day when we noticed that there was a flat for rent on our favourite street. I was living at home and he was living with friends but, carried away with the idea of living together, we decided to view the flat. I thought it was mostly for fun, but before I knew it my boyfriend was filling out forms.

He said he would pay two-thirds of the rent so that I'd only have to pay the rest. But the thing was, the 'rest' was still a lot more than nothing, which was what I was paying to live with my parents. I wanted to tell him that I couldn't afford it, but he was being so generous to offer to pay such a lot of rent that I couldn't find it in my heart to tell him no.

We moved in and I posted loads of pictures on Instagram, telling everyone about our gorgeous new flat. But I couldn't stop thinking about the fact that I was spending all my savings.

I blew through my savings in the first three months, then I got into my overdraft and took out a loan. Eventually my card was declined, and I had to tell him what was happening. He was shocked, partially at how little I was earning (we had never discussed salaries) and also because I hadn't had the confidence to tell him the truth. He felt hurt that I hadn't confided in him, I felt angry with myself for getting into debt, and the whole thing was a huge mess.

Once I admitted to him what was going on, we ended the tenancy on the super-expensive place and moved a little further out to a lovely but much cheaper place. So basically, I could have saved myself a lot of money and a lot of pain by being less afraid to offend my boyfriend, who actually wouldn't have been offended in the first place.

Mission creep

When *Dirty John* came out on Netflix, conversations about being conned became commonplace. It is not a usual situation, but it does happen, and most often to vulnerable women – specifically women who do not feel able to say no. There is a litany of reasons why a woman may feel unable to say no to someone who is asking her for money, but unquestionably the fear of being stingy, unreasonable, tight, controlling or rude is one of them.

A more common experience than deliberately being conned by someone is mission creep, where you end up paying for more and more of the costs of a relationship until eventually you are in effect supporting someone else financially. No one wants to be the girlfriend who says, 'Why haven't you offered to buy groceries recently?' or, ' Why is it me who always picks up loo roll?', but the more organised person, who sets up the accounts to pay the bills or stops at the shops on the way home from work, can end up incurring a heavy financial penalty. The only way to avoid this situation is to be open about your spending and expectations and to name the beast when you feel that someone else is not pulling their weight wallet-wise.

It's fine to support another person by taking more of the financial load, if that's a conscious choice that you have made. What you must not do is sleepwalk into being the sole provider of household essentials because you don't want to seem like a bitch for asking where the hell the money is going. In the end, anyone who is worth being in a relationship with will understand your financial barriers. Money is a very personal and often very private area, and one which you have every right to want to be discreet about. However, being discreet doesn't mean being disingenuous, nor does it justify avoiding uncomfortable conversations. If you are going to share finances with a partner then you must know their credit history and debt situation, and they yours. Similarly, if you are being asked to share the rent or mortgage on somewhere you live, you need to be extremely honest about what you can afford.

Anyone who makes you feel guilty for being blunt about money is not someone with whom to share your finances.

The right kind of rude: about money

- It is always OK to tell someone, 'I can't afford it.'

- An invitation to an event is not an obligation. If it's not in the budget then you can explain that, or you can just turn down the invite. Remember, no is a complete sentence.

- Before you share your finances with someone, ask about their debt levels and credit history. If they find this objectionable then that tells you something – and probably not something good.

- Borrowing money from friends is a recipe for disaster, but sometimes it's unavoidable. Mitigate risks by writing down your agreement and signing it. You might feel silly at the time, but it'll come in handy if there's an argument.

- Don't stretch yourself to afford something that someone else wants.

- Before you spend a significant amount of money on a wedding, hen do or any other obligation, ask yourself what you're going to get out of it and whether in a year's time you'll think that it was the right choice.

- There's nothing wrong with being stingy or tight occasionally.

- There's nothing wrong with debt – most of us have some. Refuse to feel ashamed about your debt, talk about it honestly and communicate with the body to which you owe the money and very little can go wrong. The reason debt causes pain is because we allow ourselves to be ashamed of it.

- Trust your gut. If something financial seems wrong, then it probably is. Don't be afraid to call it out.

Greta Thunberg

Greta Thunberg, born in 2003, is the most impactful teenager in the world right now. She first became known for her activism in August 2018 when, aged fifteen, she began spending her school days outside the Swedish parliament to call for stronger action on global warming by holding up a sign saying (in Swedish) 'School strike for the climate'.

Greta inspired other students, who began to engage in similar protests, which eventually became the school climate strike movement under the name 'FridaysForFuture', whereby school-aged children and teenagers don't attend school on a Friday.

There is no question that her actions have been effective. After Thunberg addressed the 2018 United Nations Climate Change Conference, student strikes took place every week somewhere in the world. In 2019, there were at least two coordinated multi-city protests involving over one million students each – pretty impressive for a movement which started with a fifteen-year-old standing outside parliament with a sign.

Predictably, despite the fact that she's a teenager asking people to take care of the planet we live on, Greta is not universally popular. In fact she seems to inspire astonishing vitriol from her critics. Grown men like Jeremy Clarkson and Toby Young cannot stand her and regularly, publicly, critique her.

Thunberg isn't the sweet, charmingly packaged starlet that we're used to seeing in famous teenagers. Her clothing is sustainable and utilitarian, she wears the same braided hairstyle from week to week and she has resisted the lure of contouring and highlighting. In an acceptance speech for the 2019 *Glamour* Woman of the Year Award, Greta described herself (via a speech read for her by Jane Fonda) as a 'nerd who has stopped shopping, refuses to fly, and who has never worn make-up or been to a hairdresser'. Greta refuses to play by the sartorial rules to which women often adhere in order to earn the right to be listened to. This seems to distress men all over the world, used as they are to listening only to sexualised women they have a low-level interest in sleeping with.

It's not just the rules of make-up and fashion that Greta disregards, either. Socially, she rejects much of the training that we as women are crippled by. Whereas most of us feel the need to say 'Thank you' three times if someone holds a door open, Greta regularly turns down awards, or uses her speech time to tell the awarding body that they should be praising climate-change scientists instead of her.

One of her most famous quotes goes as follows: 'Adults keep saying: "We owe it to the young people to give them hope." But I don't want your hope, I don't want you to be hopeful, I want you to panic. I want you to feel the fear I feel every day. And then I want you to act. I want you to act as you would in a crisis. I want you to act as if your house was on fire. Because it is.'

The whole 'You catch more flies with honey than with vinegar' thing doesn't appeal to Greta. She doesn't sugar-coat her opinions, nor does she shy away from sharing hard facts. Doubtless she would be better liked if she were willing to take a softly, softly attitude towards climate change, telling us it's not our fault but it's in our power to change. But that wouldn't be true, and Greta doesn't compromise on the truth in order to spare other people's feelings.

Greta has previously discussed how having Asperger syndrome enables her to cut through the noise, tweeting: 'I'm not public about my diagnosis to "hide" behind it, but because I know many ignorant people still see it as an "illness", or something negative. And believe me, my diagnosis has limited me before . . . I have Asperger's and that means I'm sometimes a bit different from the norm. And – given the right circumstances – being different is a superpower.'

According to Tony Attwood, who is a world authority on Asperger's, people who have ASD are 'usually renowned for being direct, speaking their mind and being honest and determined and having a strong sense of social justice'. But, as you'll probably have worked out by now, when women speak their mind they are often regarded as being rude, which is exactly why I am so in love with the idea of reclaiming the word.

There is so much that we can learn from Greta Thunberg, but most of all I see her as an inspiration in prioritising your relationship with yourself, your feelings, your politics and your values above being liked. Embracing the power of rude will mean that some people don't like you. It's not a quick or easy way to endear yourself to the world around you, but, like Greta, it's entirely possible to stop caring about that. I am yet to hear a single legitimate reason why people dislike Greta. What

I have heard is attempt after attempt to justify a hatred of her confidence, directness and rejection of hypersexualised female beauty.

It's a big ask to tell women simply to stop caring what people think of them, but Greta is a living reminder that the people who dislike you for your 'rude' behaviour are probably ones you don't want or need in your life anyway.

CHAPTER NINE

RUDE ABOUT HEALTH

During the time I was writing this book I had a miscarriage.

It started in Greece, when I was on holiday for my husband's birthday. I went to the loo, and when I wiped there were a few small spots of blood. I'd never fully understood the expression 'gripped with terror' before, but there I was, in a hotel room, feeling like the weight of the entire building was crashing around me.

We agreed there was nothing we could do. On the Internet I read that it was normal to have some bleeding in pregnancy, so I lay down on the bed (as if gravity could save the pregnancy) and read *Crazy Rich Asians* until I couldn't keep my eyes open any more. And the next morning the bleeding had stopped. Thank God, I thought.

Back in London a week later, again I went to the loo, wiped and saw a streak of blood with a few darker spots in it. I think on some level at that moment I knew. I put on my shoes, my husband ordered an Uber and we went to our nearest A&E, where upon arrival we stood in a queue for twenty minutes to get to the reception desk while I attempted not to sob.

I try to avoid complaining about the NHS because I think it is the greatest thing about the UK, but in this instance I was shocked by how cold, cavalier and careless the staff were. I explained (in hushed tones) that I was pregnant, bleeding and needed to see someone ASAP. The receptionist's face didn't register any expression and we were sent to the seating area to await triage. After some time, with nothing happening, I began to lose my mind. My phobia of seeming rude or demanding is never stronger than when I'm at a UK hospital: it's a gift to have this kind of health care; doctors are overworked and underpaid. It has been drilled into me since I was a small child that you do not complain about the NHS, so I didn't; instead I lay down on the floor, again clinging to the idea that by lying down I could avoid gravity and keep the pregnancy. Logical? Of course not. But you're not logical in that moment.

Eventually they sent doctors over to me, taking me seriously now because I was making a fuss. Gratified, I got up and went through to triage, where I was told by a cold, rude nurse that he couldn't and wouldn't help me. 'Either it's a miscarriage or it isn't,' he said. 'And we're not going to find out tonight.' I got up with as much dignity as someone who thinks she might be losing a pregnancy can possibly have, and looked him in the eye. 'I suggest that perhaps you request some further sensitivity training from your line manager,' I said. 'Because your care this evening has been less than appropriate, and you've made a very difficult experience even harder.'

I don't think I've ever used a colder voice and icier facial expression or put more venom into my words. And to this day I sometimes worry that I did the wrong thing – he'd had a long day, probably; English wasn't his first language, he might well have missed a nuance in his words – but deep down, though I feel guilty for being ungrateful to a member of NHS staff, I'm glad I said what was on my mind.

Had I not said anything I would still be fuming. What am I writing? I am still furious with him. He shrugged his shoulders over my miscarriage, as if I'd asked him if he had seen my keys or whether he wanted salami on his pizza. My little speech probably won't have changed anything, though I very much like to pretend that it did. I want to believe that next time a woman comes in with mascara tracks down her cheeks and an outfit she scrabbled together as she rushed to leave the house, he'll try to be a little kinder to her.

In reality, I very much doubt that he went ahead and asked for some sensitivity training. I doubt he even googled 'How to talk to someone who is having a miscarriage.' But I can hope. And as a result of saying something, I'm carrying around a little less anger towards him now than I would have done if I'd kept my mouth shut. I had every right to expect decent, respectful care, provided with kindness, and in that moment – one of the worst moments of my life to date – I'm proud that I practised what I preach. I was rude in a calm, moderate, practical way.

Lady problems

There are some medical problems which only affect women. Quite a lot of them, actually. Funnily enough, they seem to be the ones which are most widely ignored, misdiagnosed or brushed off as period pain.

In an episode of *Fleabag*, Kristin Scott-Thomas gives an astonishing monologue about the nature of women and pain. She tells Phoebe Waller-Bridge:

We have pain on a cycle for years and years and years and then, just when you feel you are making peace with it all, what happens? The menopause comes. The fucking menopause comes and it is the most wonderful fucking thing in the world! And, yes, your entire pelvic floor crumbles and you get fucking hot and no one cares, but then you're free. No longer a slave, no longer a machine, with parts. You're just a person in business.

And that's the thing, isn't it? If men are in pain, there is something wrong, therefore they must be taken seriously. But there is a laundry list of lady reasons that a woman might be in pain, so if she is suffering you might as well fob her off with some paracetamol because the chances are that it's nothing. Or that it's something, but that the something is just part of being a woman.

We know objectively that, when it comes to pain, men and women are treated differently. A 2008 study by the US National Institutes of Health, for example, found that women in A&E who report having acute pain are less likely to be given opioid painkillers (the most effective type) than men. When they are prescribed, women also wait longer to receive them. A 2014 study by the Institute of Medicine at the Sahlgrenska Academy found that, once they get to A&E, women wait significantly longer to see a doctor and are less often classified as an urgent case.

This can have lethal consequences. In France in May 2018, a twenty-two-year old woman named Naomi Musenga called emergency services saying her abdominal pain was so acute she felt she was 'going to die'. Instead of taking her seriously, the operator replied: 'You'll definitely die one day, like everyone else.' When the woman was taken to hospital after a five-hour wait, she had a stroke and died of multiple organ failure.

The issue of being taken seriously by doctors is by no means the fault of women. However, it does seem that we are less confident in our own assertions and more willing to be brushed off. It is common to read about women who have PCOS (poly-cystic ovary syndrome) or endometriosis – menstrual cramps are the main symptom of both – being told by a doctor that there is nothing wrong and continuing to live their lives with a chronic condition which could have been managed if the appropriate help were on offer.

Medicine is another area where women are failed worse and more often if they are not white. In 2018, black women took to Twitter to share their stories of having pain and medical issues ignored. 'It took me blacking out at work, my mom threatening the doctor who thought I was a drug addict because I was screaming from being in pain, before another doctor came and saw me. I was diagnosed with severe PCOS with a cyst the size of a grapefruit on my ovary and stage-four endometriosis,' tweeted Ashley E. Foster. 'Like Serena [Williams], I almost died of massive blood clots in my lungs and legs. The doctors initially said I just needed to lose weight. It wasn't until my blood pressure crashed to 60/20 that they finally accepted something was wrong. I was in the ICU twelve days,' posted Helena Hamilton.

It's not just anecdotal evidence either: there are multiple academic studies which demonstrate that women of colour, most of all black women, are more likely to be denied investigative medical treatment when they are ill, and less likely to be provided with the pain relief they require. A 2016 study published by the US National Academy of Sciences found that 'Black Americans are systematically undertreated for pain relative to white Americans.' Which might go some way to explaining why there is on average a seven-year age gap in life expectancy between black and white people in America.

Without a doubt, doctors need to work to overcome their biases. It is wrong that women are ignored, and even more wrong that women who aren't white are ignored for longer and more dangerously, but as non-doctors we cannot do anything about that. Our only options are to hope that we see a doctor who doesn't exhibit these prejudices or be our own advocates in demanding better and more comprehensive medical care. Yes, a person in a white coat is impressive, and it can be easy to believe them if they tell you that you're just having normal period pains or a little UTI, but you know your own body, and you know when something isn't right. So if a doctor tries to dismiss your medical problem – especially if it's a female-specific one – then that's the moment to find your inner rude. There is nothing wrong with asking for further tests or a scan to ascertain what is wrong with you. If you're wrong and it is just period pain, then fine, but if not, you've saved yourself a lot of time and pain by insisting on finding out.

One doctor, who wanted to speak to me off the record, suggested that women, especially women of colour, should attend appointments with as much 'evidence' as they can muster:

> If you have an issue which may be related to reproductive issues, then using a period-tracking app like Clue and putting as much information into it as possible will be helpful. Keeping a diary of any other symptoms, bringing a knowledge of your family's medical history, all of this will help you to be taken more seriously. You shouldn't need to, I know that. I struggle every day with the biases I see from my colleagues, towards women, towards specific racial groups. I wish it wasn't the case. But while we have to push for change, we also have to protect our patients and help them to get the best standard of care from a broken system.

Again, it is wrong that we need to do this. And more wrong still that people who aren't white need to do it better and more often, but your health is the most important thing you have. If ever there is a time to find your voice and be a rude woman, it's when you know that there is something wrong inside your body and people aren't taking it seriously.

Caren, now in her mid-fifties, started going to the doctor about her irregular periods, intense period pain and general feelings of unease about her reproductive system. 'It didn't seem to matter what I said to the doctor,' she tells me, 'they just told me that it was normal.' Ten years after her first visit, and after several more, Caren had a burst cyst during a gym class. She was rushed to hospital, put on morphine and an investigation revealed that she had a pretty dire situation in her uterus. She was told she would have to have a hysterectomy:

> I went to see a high-end male gynaecologist for a second opinion. During the consultation he told me to 'pop your knickers off', which automatically got my guard up. After he examined me, he said that yes, I did need a hysterectomy. Then he said: 'We'll get it sorted and then you can go back to using it for what it's intended!' then sent me on my way. I left the room dazed, unable to believe that a medical professional would say anything so callous after telling you that you needed to have a major organ removed. Of course, I didn't say anything, but to this day I cannot stand the man.

Period pain

When I was a teenager, I would occasionally have a period so painful that I would throw up, and then spend the entire day in bed clutching a hot-water bottle. At no point did anyone ever suggest that I needed to see a doctor about this, so I just assumed that it was a normal part of adulthood and got on with it without making much fuss. Years later it transpired that I had one polycystic ovary and a minor fibroid, which might have accounted for the hideousness of my period pains. I'd have known this a lot earlier if I'd thought to make a big deal about the pain, but that just isn't what women do.

For those of us with chronic period pain, it's a case of dragging yourself through life for three to seven days a month without making a fuss, because who could bring themselves to make a fuss? We carry tampons up our sleeves on the way to the loo at work and tell our bosses that we're 'under the weather' when we mean bleeding from the vagina, and we accept pain as a basic part of being a woman. Unfortunately, period pain is a cover-all for medical professionals looking at a person with a uterus and is often used as the reason why we don't get better or more accurate treatment faster.

We need to be able to say to a medical professional who is not taking our period pain seriously: 'I realise that there is an element of normality in having painful periods, but there is also a history of women dying or becoming seriously ill because their health issues were assumed to be menstrual cramps, and I do not want to add to their number.'

We also need to become comfortable with cluing in our employers if we have health issues related to our menstrual cycle; 3.8 per cent of women have missed work or school because of their period, but most of them report that they felt unable to be honest about the reason. Of the women who have called in sick on their period, just under 80% gave their employer or school a more general excuse instead.

The pill

When the pill was invented it was widely considered to be a miracle, one of the greatest inventions of the twentieth century. A true step forward for women all over the world, and a turning point in civilisation. For the first time, women would be able to make an active choice as to whether or not they wanted to become pregnant. Women were going to be able to have babies on their own timetable, and they were even going to be able to enjoy recreational sex. Unfortunately, since that miracle came along, very little about it has changed.

We as women are supposed to be as grateful in 2020 as we were in the 1960s, when the pill was rolled out across the UK to married women, and then eventually on demand, despite the fact that it has a litany of side effects – the full complement of which are as follows:

- intermenstrual spotting
- nausea
- breast tenderness
- depression
- headaches or migraines
- weight gain
- mood swings
- missed periods
- decreased libido
- vaginal discharge
- changes to eyesight for people who wear contact lenses
- in rare cases, blood clots and strokes

On top of this riot of fun, the pill is also linked to certain types of cancer, specifically cervical cancer. When I first went on the pill my GP told me: 'It makes you more likely to get cervical cancer, but a bit less likely to get breast cancer, so it kind of works out as an even split!' and then gave a jolly little laugh. Apparently, the best we can expect from a medication that we take every day is that it only slightly raises our risk of cervical cancer. Lucky fucking us.

Make no mistake, the pill might have been a miracle for women in the 1960s, but it's also not a very nice drug. The most compelling proof of this is that the original researchers tested the contraceptive pill on female prisoners in Puerto Rico and mentally ill women in the US, because the women in their drug trials kept dropping out due to horrific side effects.

Compare that to today, when the 2016 drug trials of a male contraceptive pill had to cease because several men had slight headaches.

While the headache drug trial cessation rankles with me, I can't help wondering if the men have the right idea: a drug that you take every day to avoid pregnancy shouldn't involve giving you a headache. The only thing that the contraceptive pill should do is prevent you from getting pregnant – and possibly I'd be open to a hair and nail supplement or a multivitamin – but perhaps we, like the men in the drug trials, should refuse to take medication which can make us feel miserable, sexless and depressed while giving us weight gain, mood swings and bigger boobs. Maybe if we had been a little ruder about the whole thing there would have been more innovation in the development of better female contraceptives. Markets respond to demand, and we've all been docilely swallowing pills developed almost sixty years ago because we're just so lucky not to be getting pregnant each month.

How have we, as an entire 51 per cent of the species, allowed a situation where a medication we take to avoid pregnancy gives us this litany of horrible side effects? We've been so sodding polite about the whole thing that we're not getting a fair deal.

In 2013, fed up with the way that the contraceptive pill made me feel, and sick of the process of attending the doctor's office every three months to be assessed for another prescription, I decided that I was done with the pill. I'd given it five years, let it make me moody, miserable and sexless, and there was no point in sticking with it. Instead I told my brand-new boyfriend (now husband) that we would be using condoms.

Whenever I tell women this, they wrinkle their noses and say, 'And he agreed to that?!' To which I reply, 'I find most men prefer sex with a condom to no sex at all.' I know that unprotected sex feels better (refer back to the rude sex chapter for more on condoms), and using the fertility planning method I've been able to have quite a lot of it, but for times when I'm fertile we use a condom, and I refuse to be made to feel guilty about that. Why should my health and happiness suffer on a daily basis for an activity which takes place (in my case) three to five times a week? And if a man you're contemplating having sex with doesn't want to use a condom, in other words doesn't allow you to make comfortable choices about contraceptives, then maybe he's not someone you should be having sex with in the first place.

The moment they make a contraceptive pill which doesn't make me feel sick, miserable, give me swollen boobs or kill my sex drive I'll be delighted to take it, but until then I'll be refusing to do so, because I'm not going to sacrifice my health and happiness on the altar of someone else's orgasm.

The morning-after pill

I have taken the morning-after pill seven or eight times in my life – not because I am irresponsible, but because I am extremely responsible. Every time I've had even the slightest chance of a contraceptive mishap, I have found my way to a chemist to procure emergency contraception. As such, I am very familiar with the consultation process which goes on when you attempt to buy it. First of all you have a fun back-and-forth when you try to tell the chemist behind the counter that you want the morning-after pill without everyone in the shop turning to have a look at the Jezebel in the scarlet letter (yes, I'm mixing my slut-shaming metaphors). Then you're taken into a little room for a 'consultation', which the British Pregnancy Advisory Service (BPAS) have stated is not medically necessary. The consultation can be, in my experience, more of a telling-off than a medical assessment. There is an argument that the chemist might helpfully ask about your cycle or your blood pressure, but I've had chemists ask whether I used a condom; whether the condom 'really' split; if the person I was having sex with was my boyfriend. I was once even asked how old my boyfriend was. The first couple of times this happened I was furious, but obedient: I regarded the lecture about safe sex as my punishment, the price I had to pay for the medication I needed (alongside the very expensive actual price, which we'll come to in a moment).

The last time I took the morning-after pill I was in my late twenties; I'd been writing about women's healthcare and reproductive rights for a long time, so I knew what, if anything, the chemist needed to ask and went fully armed into the consultation room with the judgemental man in the white coat.

'What contraception were you using?' he asked me. 'That's not relevant,' I told him. 'Do you want to know the details of my cycle?' He looked aghast, but he prescribed the medicine I needed and for the first time I left a chemist feeling not like a stupid, scolded child but like a competent adult.

Back in 2017, BPAS mounted a campaign to get retailers to sell the morning-after pill (otherwise known as emergency contraception or Plan B) for a lower price. It was originally retailing at between £30 and £40 – a huge amount of money for anyone who is on a low income, and a price that made a lot of women, especially very young or very poor women, decide to risk an unplanned pregnancy. BPAS pointed out that in other European countries, the pill costs about £8 and can be bought over the counter. One journalist from *Vice* took a bus from London to Paris and bought the morning-after pill to demonstrate that it was actually cheaper to buy it in France, even if you had to travel there to get it.

Eventually one high street chemist, Superdrug, took the complaints seriously and released a generic-brand emergency contraceptive you could buy for £13.49, which was still more than it cost in other countries but a step in the right direction. Boots, however, decided that they didn't want to drop the price of their hormonal contraceptives. Clare Murphy, Director of External Affairs for BPAS, wrote to them to find out why. Rather than the generalised fobbing-off you would expect from a major high street retailer, Clare received a more detailed answer. 'In our experience,' wrote Marc Donavan, the Chief Pharmacist at Boots, 'the subject of emergency hormonal contraception polarises public opinion and we receive frequent contact from individuals who voice their disapproval at the fact that the company chooses to provide this service. We would not want to be accused of incentivising inappropriate use, and provoking complaints, by significantly reducing the price of this product.'

When I read Donavan's comment, back in 2017, I felt like throwing a chair through a window. I had taken the morning-after pill six or seven times at that point, and his brazen slut-shaming really felt like he was taking aim at me (and at all women who needed emergency contraception during their years of sexual activity). The BPAS states that there is no reason why the morning-after pill should be avoided, no limit on how often you can take it and no logical or scientific reason for the stigma which surrounds it. Women all over the UK were rightly incensed, and what happened next was the perfect demonstration of the power of rude. People tweeted, emailed, phoned and even wrote to Boots to express their frustration. It was national news. Then in November, more than 130 MPs wrote to Boots UK's Managing Director, Elizabeth Fagan, to demand that the £15.99 version go on sale immediately, with senior Labour figures accusing the company of failing to uphold women's reproductive rights in not supplying cheap contraceptive pills in all its stores. Six months later Boots capitulated, and the significantly cheaper version of the pill is now in stores nationwide. Clearly, when we put our minds to it and get rude, we are capable of effecting change on a massive scale.

Miscarriages

There are different types of miscarriage: some of them happen 'naturally', and some need intervention. Mine was the latter. It's sometimes called a 'missed' miscarriage because your body doesn't expel the pregnancy and continues to make pregnancy hormones – though the word 'missed' feels rather blamey so we're encouraged not to use it. Anyway, because of the nature of my miscarriage, I had to have medication – two pills inserted at the neck of my vagina – to make my uterus contract and expel the pregnancy tissue. Unfortunately, this didn't totally work. It turns out that my body isn't very good at having a miscarriage, and I was left with some tissue at the top right-hand corner of my uterus, which made the extraction more complicated. I asked the kindly doctor who explained this to me whether it meant that I had tissue in the worst possible location, and he responded by saying, 'We don't like to use the word "worst".' I took his response as a yes.

Four weeks passed between finding I had miscarried and having the surgery, with the pills in the middle. It was (and, for full disclosure, this is only a couple of weeks from time of writing) one of the worst times of my life. As an added extra, I started having nightmares. Vivid, long dreams about objects – lengths of plastic tubing mostly – falling out of my vagina covered in blood. Or, even worse, I was giving birth to a tiny but perfectly lifelike baby doll. Suffice to say, I wasn't having much fun. Several medical professionals replied to my comments about these dreams by telling me that it sounded like PTSD. I brushed off their comments because PTSD is for people who've been to war zones – not people who've had miscarriages. That's the funny thing about a miscarriage: you're left to look after yourself, you go to the bathroom and feel large chunks of tissue falling out of your vagina, and then you wash your hands and get on with it.

I went to a wedding the day that my miscarriage was in full force. I've never felt more ill or more sad, but I smiled and drank cocktails and put on a show. Halfway through the afternoon my underwear became unable to support the size of sanitary towel required for my bleeding, so I asked my husband for his – he spent the rest of the day commando, while I wore his boxer briefs. In retrospect, it was complete madness not to stay at home, crying and bleeding in private, but I didn't make much of a fuss because I'd never known anyone else to make a fuss about a miscarriage, so it seemed that this was just what you were supposed to do.

According to Maternity Action, women are not entitled to any formal miscarriage leave. They explain:

> If you need time off work following the loss of your baby you can ask your employer if they provide compassionate leave or you could ask to take annual leave or agree a period of unpaid leave.
>
> You are entitled to take sick leave if you are not well enough to work and you should follow your employer's sickness reporting procedures. If you need time off sick as a result of your miscarriage this should be treated as pregnancy-related sickness; however, it is a good idea to talk to your GP as it is up to your GP to certify whether your absence is pregnancy-related.
>
> If your sick leave is certified as pregnancy or miscarriage-related that will apply for as long as your sick leave lasts.
>
> The Equality Act 2010 provides protection against discrimination on the grounds of pregnancy or pregnancy-related sickness for a protected period of two weeks from the end of a pregnancy for women who are not entitled to maternity leave. During this period, you are protected against discrimination related to your pregnancy, miscarriage or related sick leave.

So basically, if you lose a pregnancy before twenty-four weeks (six months) then you might get two weeks off if your doctor signs the form; other than that you'll be expected to go back to work and get on with it.

*

I'm a freelance writer with an extremely understanding editor who treated me as if I were made of glass in the wake of my loss, letting me write about it as much or as little as I wanted to, and not raising an eyebrow when I said I wasn't able to come into work. Most women are not so lucky.

I can't imagine how humiliating it would have been to have begged time off for a doctor's appointment to ask a GP to sign off on being allowed two weeks' sick leave to grieve for the loss of a much-wanted pregnancy, but that's what women have to do. And if the doctor says no, you just go back to work. Never mind if you're still bleeding, still seething with pregnancy hormones, still bursting into tears every time you see a targeted advert on Instagram for maternity wear. You get on with it.

I had intended to include a link to a petition for women to be given automatic miscarriage leave. But I couldn't find one, because at time of writing there wasn't one.

As far as I can tell, the main reason why women aren't entitled to miscarriage leave without first convincing their GP that they need it, and why there is no move to change this, is that women going through the aftermath of a miscarriage don't really feel like campaigning to change the law. I've never felt less like being rude than I did after my miscarriage. Being rude takes time. Effort. Fight. All of which had been knocked out of my body. But, as is the case with so much female health care, it's a vicious circle. We don't demand more, and because we don't demand it, we don't get it. We might talk to our friends about our frustrations, or reflect on how unfair it is to have to go back to work after a pregnancy loss, or take a pill every day that makes us anxious and miserable, but we swallow it down anyway. And so nothing changes.

Fat shaming

When I went for my first maternity appointment, I was terrified: I'd put on half a stone in seven weeks of pregnancy because I was so madly hungry all the time, and, having given up smoking and drinking cold-turkey, I felt I needed something to get me through. I'd heard horror story after horror story about being told off for weight gain, and, having spent much of my teenage years bingeing and purging, I was not in the mood for a relapse-triggering lecture about my weight. To my enormous delight, when I arrived at the clinic and was handed over to my midwife, I found that she was a very full-figured, very tall woman who presumably wasn't obsessed with weight. She certainly didn't say a cross word about mine.

I'm a UK size 14–16, depending on how close to Christmas we are, so my personal experience of medicalised fat shaming is limited. I'm sure if I asked my GP whether I should lose some weight she would say yes, as I am overweight. However, in all the time that I have spent in hospital, which has been quite a lot recently, I've never had anyone comment on my weight or suggest that it requires management. Unfortunately, this is not the case for lots of plus-size women, especially women who are at the higher end of the weight spectrum. When you are not thin passing (an expression used to describe women like me who are not thin, but are not fat in a noticeable way), having a doctor blame absolutely everything on your weight is a common experience.

Jess is twenty-four. 'I'm a size 24–26,' she tells me, 'and whenever I go to the doctor, even for something completely unrelated, it's the first thing that they tell me. I had a series of really strong headaches and the first suggestion was weight loss. It turned out that what I actually needed was glasses.'

PMS and PMDD

I've always struggled with PMS (premenstrual syndrome). Ever since my periods started, I can directly track the relationship between my mood and my cycle. When I'm ovulating, I'm sunny and sweet; the week before my period, I'm angry, impatient, snappish and often really deeply miserable. As a teenager, I went to the doctor to discuss this and was relieved when she laughed. 'That's just being a woman, I'm afraid,' she told me. And, rather than questioning the idea that I was going to spend the rest of my life feeling miserable one week in four, I felt stupid. Being a woman meant suffering – I had worked that part out. Pain was part of the process. Why on earth was I making a silly fuss? It was only years later that I learned about PMDD, which stands for premenstrual dysphoric disorder, and started to wonder if my PMS might be something darker.

PMDD is a severe form of PMS, which can cause both emotional and physical symptoms every month during the week or two before you start your period. It's like PMS with the volume turned up to 100. The symptoms of PMDD include:

- mood swings
- feeling upset or tearful
- feeling angry or irritable
- feeling anxious
- feeling hopeless
- feeling tense or on edge
- difficulty concentrating
- feeling overwhelmed
- lack of energy

- less interest in activities you normally enjoy
- suicidal feelings
- breast tenderness or swelling
- pain in your muscles and joints
- headaches
- feeling bloated
- changes in your appetite such as overeating or having specific food cravings
- sleep problems
- finding it hard to avoid or resolve conflicts with people around you
- becoming very upset if you feel that others are rejecting you

Long list, isn't it? Given what a miserable experience PMDD is, you'd think there would be a whole range of things on offer to help those suffering with it, right? Not so much.

Years after my original visit, I went to my GP to talk about the fact that while my mood was even and reasonably positive most of the month, in the week before my period I was having all the symptoms of depression. She informally diagnosed me with PMDD. It was sort of a relief. Unlike the first visit, when I'd thought I was being a fussy brat, this time I felt understood. It wasn't just silly old lady brain making me mad, and it wasn't just a lack of self-control making me short-tempered and snappy; there was something legitimately wrong.

'So, what can we do?' I asked the doctor. She looked almost guilty as she told me that the answer was 'pretty much nothing'. If you've got PMS or PMDD, the options are as follows:

- You can go on the pill, which comes with its own problems, doesn't suit all women and doesn't always work.

- You can try talking therapy, but as it's a chemical, hormonal issue this might not work.

- You can take antidepressants all month to treat an issue that only affects you for five to seven days.

- In extreme cases, you can opt for a full hysterectomy, which means being unable to have children (or any more children) and have to take hormone replacement therapy (HRT) until you're ready to experience the menopause.

- Or, finally, you take something called Gonadotropin-releasing hormone (GnRH), which can relieve PMDD symptoms by bringing on a temporary menopause. It typically comes in the form of injections or a nasal spray. The most fun thing about that is that taking it can cause side effects such as loss of bone density, which puts you at higher risk of developing osteoporosis (a condition in which your bones become weak and break more easily).

Is it any wonder that, given the lack of suitable options on offer, most women just put up with feeling miserable one week a month?

Natalie, twenty-four, told me:

My doctor offered me various options. Antidepressants didn't work for me, going on the pill did nothing. GnRH wasn't an option as I already have bone density issues, so now I just feel suicidal for five days in any one month, and try to remind myself that it will pass and that I will feel normal again once my period arrives.

My GP told me that some women find their hormones rebalance after they have a pregnancy. I'm thinking I might fast-track having kids when I'm in a relationship and hope that that works. Honestly, at this point I would try almost anything to feel normal for four weeks in a row.

As with the pill, and with the menopause, the lack of treatment for PMDD and PMS is down to a perceived lack of need. Instead of being seen as a cruel torture of nature, PMS is a punchline. We make jokes about sitting in bed sobbing at adverts featuring cute puppies rather than demanding that someone puts time and money into finding a cure. We don't make a huge fuss about the misery that our hormones can cause us, so nothing is done about it.

Giving birth

'When I'm in labour,' I said to some friends recently, 'I'm not going to let anyone put anything inside me before they've at least introduced themselves.' Everyone around the table who had already given birth laughed, as if I'd announced that I would be having my baby removed by laser while someone gave me a head massage. This 'Oh you've got no idea' response has, generally speaking, been my experience of expressing any feelings about labour or pregnancy as a child-free woman. 'That's not how it works,' the friends at this dinner told me. 'One nurse told me that I should pop my dignity by the door. I had people putting their hands in my vagina without even saying a word to me first,' said another friend.

When I expressed horror at the idea of having someone put their hand inside my body without my consent, several of the women at the gathering seemed frustrated, telling me, 'It's not about how you feel, it's about having a healthy baby.' Apparently, I am unreasonable to think it's a bit medieval to have to choose between a healthy baby or retaining some control over how you give birth.

*

In 2018, when Meghan Markle was pregnant with her first child, Archie, she came under intense scrutiny for her plans to give birth on her own terms. The first transgression came in the form of an announcement that she wouldn't be doing the post-birth photoshoot outside the hospital, à la Diana and Kate. Then it was the fact that she apparently passed over the traditional royal-birth medical team for a female doctor, saying that she didn't want her labour run by 'men in suits' (I love you Meghan).

For some reason, all of these perfectly reasonable choices made people furious. How dare the duchess try to choose how her baby is born? For my part, I had been largely neutral about her as a person before this, but I became something of a super-fan as a result of her attitude to becoming a mum.

I'm not stupid. I, like most women, realise that labour isn't generally a fun experience, but is it really so unreasonable to expect decent treatment? Much of the commentary around Markle's birth focused on her being 'ungrateful' for the top-tier care she had been offered. Critics went so far as to call her a 'brat'. But honestly, if being a 'brat' is how you get full control of the way in which you give birth, then sign me up. I would be delighted to be a birth 'brat'. It seems that if you are not a birth 'brat', then your chances of getting the birth you want and deserve are pretty low.

It is short-sighted to discuss the way in which Meghan Markle is treated by the press and the general public without acknowledging the inherent racism she contends with day to day. Would a white woman have been given quite such a hard time for wanting to choose her own birth plan?

The 'angry black woman' stereotype has been written about extensively, both in academic studies and in terms of personal essays. In 2014, Wendy Ashley laid out an explanation of the trope in a paper titled 'The angry black woman: the impact of pejorative stereotypes on psychotherapy with black women'. She writes: 'In the aftermath of slavery and the resulting social, economic, and political effects, Black women have become the victims of negative stereotyping in mainstream American culture. Such stereotypes include the myth of the angry Black woman that characterizes these women as aggressive, ill-tempered, illogical, overbearing, hostile, and ignorant without provocation.'

We can't know how much of the treatment of Meghan Markle during pregnancy was down to racist stereotyping, but what we do know is that black women in the UK are five times more likely to die during childbirth as white women, so if any group deserves to demand the highest possible standard of care, it is women of colour.

As is so often the case when we talk about the female experience, being a woman is hard, but being a woman of colour is harder still. Candice Brathwaite is a blogger and writer; she nearly died of sepsis shortly after she gave birth to her daughter, despite having been reassured by medical professionals that she was 'fine'. She wrote an article for *Grazia Daily* in which she said:

> Although the dismal maternal mortality rates for African-American women have long since been made public, aside from peer-to-peer conversation, Black British women like myself had no data or evidence to depend on. Until now.
>
> Having the data to hand made me braver about stating what I thought the issue had been all along, and it was that the poor treatment was most definitely rooted in racial bias. From the moment I went to the doctor (who incorrectly assumed I was a single mother) up until during my induced labour, when one of the midwives chastised me for not being 'strong enough', all of

these microaggressions, judgements and the flippant treatment were entirely down to the fact that I was a black woman.

What Brathwaite hits on here is a tendency that we women have, against which women of colour have the biggest battle: to wait until we have insurmountable evidence that we are right before we feel entitled to act, especially those of us who come from marginalised groups or minorities, people who are used to being gaslighted and told that their experiences aren't real. Yes, 'proving' your point is essential if you're campaigning for change or taking part in a formal debate, but in your daily life it's OK to act based on your sense of the world and your feelings about how you are being treated, without having a lever arch file of statistics to hand every time you open your mouth.

A word that was used a lot to describe Meghan Markle during her pregnancy was 'entitled'. When she dismissed the 'men in suits' in the royal medical team she was being selfish. When she (allegedly) favoured a home birth over the Lindo Wing of St Mary's hospital, where Harry and William were born, she was being spoiled. But here's the thing: Meghan, like every other woman in the UK, was literally entitled – entitled to choose how she gave birth.

Did you know that women are permitted to request elective C-sections? I have read thread after thread on Mumsnet about how to 'convince' your doctor to 'allow' you to have a C-section, when women are fully and completely entitled to one if they choose. No hoop-jumping, no convincing anyone. Women also have the right to refuse induction, and to demand as much or as little pain relief as is safe to take; and yet there are women all over the UK who don't know that they can make their own choices about how they give birth, not by wheedling and convincing doctors to allow it, but by being the right kind of rude and saying, 'I know I am entitled to do this the way I want to do it, please help me to make the decision which is best for me and my baby.'

Birth rape, or obstetric violence, is the term used to describe a situation when a woman is subjected to a non-consensual vaginal examination during labour. The term was first used legally in Venezuela, when it was brought into legislation in 2007 to protect women giving birth. It is illegal in Argentina and in Mexico, but not currently in the UK.

I don't have children yet, but I'm hoping to in the near future, which is why I've already started coaching my husband on how to tell a doctor that I don't want an internal examination and to read up on my legal rights to a Caesarean or to resist an induction. If and when I get there, I will probably also hire a doula to represent my interests and needs during childbirth. I shouldn't need to, but it's too important an experience to risk being ignored. The NHS is a marvel – we are lucky to have it – but medical staff are fallible, just like all humans are. It's easy to stop seeing patients as people, and that's when birth rape happens. As is so often true of the way in which women are treated, there is an expectation that we should be so grateful to be in labour that our bodily autonomy ceases to matter. That expectation can absolutely go fuck itself.

Having someone penetrate your body without your consent is not permissible outside of the labour ward. It does not magically become acceptable because you are in labour. You do not have to accept it because you are grateful to be getting medical attention. Women aren't stupid. They're not asking for a magic wand to make labour feel like a deep-tissue massage. We are perfectly aware that labour is a painful, arduous and physically destructive process, but that's no excuse for medical practitioners to add to the burden by penetrating women without their consent. If that happens to you, you have every right to be furious. You do not have to accept medicalised assault as part and parcel of having a baby.

Whether it's a home birth or an elective C-section, you have a right to give birth in the way you want, or at least to give it a go. If ever there is a time to discover the power of rude, it's during pregnancy. The system is old-fashioned and sees the only important outcome as you and your baby surviving. It's OK to want more than survival. It's OK to want to make plans and have those plans respected, just as it's OK to change your mind part of the way through. In no other gruelling medical ordeal would you be expected to smile and act like you're lucky.

The menopause

After several decades of period pains, mood swings and the fear of leaking blood on a white sofa, you are rewarded with the menopause. The menopause is an enormous medical experience. The symptoms associated with it can be brutal, miserable and life-ruining. As a result of the combination of hot flushes, mood swings, insomnia and night sweats, 25 per cent of women reported having symptoms of depression during their menopause. Despite the massive discomfort that can accompany the menopause, women have always been expected simply to get on with it.

But the horrors of the menopause are often simply laughed off like a punchline or an insult; it's just part of getting older and fair game for a gag. We describe women as 'menopausal', as lazy shorthand for middle-aged, shopping at Marks and Spencer and small-c conservative; it's a concept associated with comfortable shoes and stretchy trousers. Sadly, it's also a time in a woman's life when she can be written off: she's no longer useful for giving birth, she may not be as sexually alluring as she once was, and is therefore ignored or laughed at. Just as with periods, because it's a 'lady problem' we draw a veil over it rather than addressing it directly.

Medical science has done some astonishing things: we can replace organs with donor ones; keep people artificially alive via machines; and cure diseases that would have been a death sentence even a couple of decades ago. And yet beyond the invention of HRT, which was a revolution but took place in 1942, no progress has been made in helping women through one of the best-known natural phenomena in the female experience.

Every woman who lives into her seventies will go through menopause, so 50 per cent of the population who make it to old age go through it; but apart from some hormonal remedies and the blunt instrument of HRT, there's really not much that can be done to ease the transition, because most women have not demanded it, and those who did have been ignored.

In October 2019, Channel 4 announced that women employees would be given the option of taking menopause leave. A month later the Labour Party stated that, if it was in government, it would give menopause leave to all women. Whether or not we need menopause leave is a debate between women. For some, the idea of being able to step back from the workplace to experience this brutal hormonal bullying would be essential. However, some feminist thinkers, including Julie Burchill, have suggested that removing women from the workplace due to womb-related issues is quite Victorian-sounding, patronising and even a danger to women's progress.

Whether you believe that we should be able to have menopause leave or not, there is no doubt that as a medical phenomenon the menopause is under-researched and very much ignored. Once again women are left alone to wrestle with hideous side effects with little support.

It gets better

Reading about the menopause was pretty shocking, I won't lie. I had assumed it was a handful of hot flushes and then the joy of being done with your periods for ever. Not so. That said, the ageing process does seem to come with some serious benefits.

One of the most reassuring aspects of the *Rude* survey was that women consistently said they had become ruder as they got older. Getting older seemed to have provided women with more confidence, more aggression and less concern about what people thought of them. Possibly that's down to the process of gaining more wisdom (observing what happens to you, the demanding what you want and prioritising your wants and needs above seeming sweet). There were dozens of stories about things that happened to women in their teens or twenties which ended with, 'But I would never allow that to happen to me now.' So we're taught as little girls that we're not supposed to be rude, we spend our adult lives unlearning that lesson and finish up in our middle to late age with a healthy disdain for it.

Some women told me that getting ruder as they got older was about no longer being seen as a sex object. 'I always wanted men to see me as feminine and approachable,' says Catherine. 'But I'm nearly fifty now and, while I still take care about my appearance, I'm not going to be an ingénue any more, so I let myself be ballsier. And to be honest, it's a lot more fun.'

The right kind of rude: about health

- Your health is one of the most precious resources that you have, so wanting to look after it is not unreasonable.

- Because health care is free in the UK, it can be harder to demand the standard of care that you require. However, medical professionals are still fallible, and therefore if you suspect that they are overlooking something important, you need to make that point until you are heard.

- If you don't feel that medical staff are listening to you or treating you in a productive way, then you can request a change of doctor.

- Taking data and evidence when you meet with your doctor can help them to understand that you require their help. This is especially valuable in terms of data concerning your menstrual cycle. There are dozens of apps which will allow you to chart this.

- Do not settle for a form of birth control which makes you feel unwell within yourself. Keep going back until you find something which works for you, or use condoms. There is nothing wrong with only using protection when you are actually having sex.

- Many experts claim that periods should not be painful at all, so if yours are extremely painful, don't just write it off with a hot-water bottle and some painkillers. Get answers. There may well be a reason why you are in such pain.

- Similarly, if you have itching, burning or anything else unpleasant going on with your vulva or vagina, don't just assume it's a yeast infection and get on with it. It's worth a trip to the doctor.

• Nothing about your body is wrong or gross. Illness is not a weakness or a fault, no matter how you contracted it. You deserve good-quality, effective medical care from a medical practitioner who treats you with kindness.

Tallulah Bankhead

Tallulah Brockman Bankhead (1902–68) was an American stage and screen actress. She was a member of a prominent Alabama political family. Her grandfather and uncle were both US Senators and her father served as member of Congress. However, despite her family's political affiliations, which tended towards being conservative, Tallulah supported causes such as civil rights. She often opposed her own family publicly, but that was only the beginning of her rude behaviour.

Tallulah had the kind of healthy sexual appetite which wasn't commonly expressed by women of her background during the early twentieth century. She was unapologetically bi-sexual (though she preferred the term 'ambisexterous') and was famous for having a lot of sex with both men and women. In 1932, during an interview with *Motion Picture* magazine, she said: 'I'm serious about love. I'm damned serious about it now ... I haven't had an affair for six months. Six months! Too long ... If there's anything the matter with me now, it's not Hollywood or Hollywood's state of mind ... The matter with me is, I WANT A MAN! . . . Six months is a long, long while. I WANT A MAN!'

Following the release of the first Kinsey Report (which explored human sexual attraction on a scale from one to six) she commented, 'I found no surprises in the Kinsey Report. The good doctor's clinical notes were old hat to me . . . I've had many momentary love affairs. A lot of these impromptu romances have been climaxed in a fashion not generally condoned. I go into them impulsively. I scorn any notion of their permanence. I forget the fever associated with them when a new interest presents itself.'

Perhaps the most appealing thing about her was her total lack of apology. In 1933 she nearly died following a five-hour emergency hysterectomy due to venereal disease. Weighing only seventy pounds when she left hospital, she stoically said to her doctor, 'Don't think this has taught me a lesson!' Before the hysterectomy Bankhead had previously had four abortions, at a time when abortion was still technically illegal.

She died aged sixty-six due to double pneumonia, caused in part by her chain-smoking (she was said to smoke 150 cigarettes a day). Her last words were allegedly, 'Codeine . . . bourbon.'

Her unapologetic attitude towards her own health – she was not ashamed of those medical conditions which arose as a result of enjoying her life – serves as a lesson to those of us who can't even bring ourselves to tell our GP how many units of alcohol we drink each week. Bankhead didn't 'mea culpa' for needing medical treatment as the result of living a passionate, sexual life. Instead she smiled through the consequences and got on with it.

FINAL THOUGHTS

As I have mentioned, the first thing I did when I started writing *The Power of Rude* was to keep a diary of my day, looking for examples of my fear. So it felt fitting that, as I came to the end of the writing process, I would do it again and see how things had changed.

9 a.m.
I take the Tube to work. On the platform people try to push past me to get onto the train but I hold fast – not pushing back, but not letting them move me. When we get on the train people are squashed by the doors even though there is space in the middle. Usually I would ignore the problem while silently seething with my face up against the glass, or passive-aggressively say, 'Can we move down please?' Today I move down, and, to my surprise, other people follow me. I arrive at work without the sense of anger that always comes from Tube wars.

9.35 a.m.
I am very slightly late for a meeting – only by a minute or two. I decided to take my own advice from the work chapter and, instead of piling into the meeting apologising for my ineptitude, I sit down and say, 'Thank you so much for waiting for me,' and then we begin. It could just be my imagination, but it seems people are listening more closely to my ideas.

11 a.m.

I go into another meeting to discuss an ongoing project. The person on the other side of the table wants me to put together a campaign with very little notice and no budget. I tell her that it's not really an option: instead of spending days trying to make it work and then having to deliver the news that it won't, I've gone down the expectation management route. She is frustrated and not wildly pleased about it, but I leave the meeting knowing that I haven't made my own life more difficult and feel glad.

1 p.m.

I'm so hungry that my concentration is slipping, and I need to eat. Someone asks if I can pop into a meeting for half an hour. 'I need to eat something first,' I say, overwhelmed by my own bravery. Traditionally I've just skipped lunch or drunk a Diet Coke and hoped that it would fill me up. Half an hour later I'm back at my desk with a renewed ability to concentrate. I join the end of the meeting and I like to think I was quite helpful.

3 p.m.

I have to finish writing an article by 4 p.m. but one of my close friends who lives abroad is having problems. She sends me a stream of messages. Rather than go into a meeting room, WhatsApp her for as long as she needs and then stay late to finish the article (and everything else that needs doing), I channel my inner Melissa Fabello. I'm practically having heart palpitations as I send a message saying, 'I'm just in the middle of something, can we Skype later? Maybe over a glass of wine?' Her reply is a little terse, but I file the article on time.

5 p.m.
I get a message from some school friends about a bottomless brunch they want to go to. It costs £45 a head and it's all Prosecco (which I don't like). I tell them that it's not my thing but that I'd love to see them soon and, amazingly, other people start to concur. We all agree to skip the bottomless brunch but book in a drink in a few days' time.

5.30 p.m.
I have finished working, so without asking anyone I pack up my things. 'I've been productive today,' I say as I put on my coat. 'See you all tomorrow.'

7.00 p.m.
My husband comes home, and I suggest that, as I've cooked all week, maybe he could pop some sausages in the oven and make some mashed potato. He's very happy to do so and even makes onion gravy. It's delicious and I tell him so. He says that he's really enjoying getting into cooking and that he had previously assumed that I wouldn't have 'let' him. I realise that in my attempts to be an amazing partner, I'd been setting great food on the table every night for the last six years, but I'd also been depriving him of the chance to enjoy learning to put meals together.

9.00 p.m.
I say that I want to watch *Succession*. My husband doesn't, so he has a bath and reads in bed for a while. When I come to bed, he tells me that he likes this new routine we've fitted into. 'I like the fact that I never have to guess what you want or what you're thinking any more,' he tells me.

11 p.m.

Husband is snoring again – worse than ever. I decide to go and sleep in our spare room. It's hard to shake the feeling that we're failing at being married if we don't share a bedroom, but when the snoring is really bad, I need to sleep somewhere else. I've been doing it once or twice a week since I finished writing *The Power of Rude*, and in the morning I wake up happier and more refreshed. Often I'll get up around six and go back to bed with him for a while, so that we still get to lie tangled up together before the alarm goes off.

I was genuinely surprised by the change in my attitude to the world around me, and by how different it has made me feel. For a word so steeped in negative association, it's incredible how happy being rude can make you feel.

Many times while writing *The Power of Rude* I felt that the examples I gave were too small, too bitty or too insignificant to mean much. But that's the thing about being afraid to be rude: it doesn't ruin your life in a matter of days, weeks or even months, it's death by a thousand cuts. Every time someone pushes you and you don't say 'Hey!', every time you apologise for something that isn't your fault, every time you put your own wants and needs at the bottom of a long list, below everyone else's, it builds up. And eventually it starts to squeeze your life harder and tighter, until the defining characteristic about you is that you try never to offend or annoy anyone around you.

Your hallmark should be what you did, not what you didn't do. An absence of something is not a goal. Attempting to live in a way in which you do not cause pain or harm to others is noble, but it's essential at the same time to attempt to live a life that makes you feel happy, valued, seen and heard. Achieving that is a whole lot harder – perhaps even impossible – if you walk through the world terrified that people are going to think that you are rude.

Writing this book has been more therapeutic than I could have anticipated. I have laid to rest the ghosts of things I have done, or not done, said or not had the courage to say; ghosts that have followed me for years. I think perhaps most of us are similarly haunted, like the ultimate version of the French *l'esprit de l'escalier*. There have been times in the writing of *The Power of Rude* that it has seemed like a catalogue of female failures, which will do my gender no favours at all, and there have been moments when I've been genuinely frustrated by my own sex and I've wanted to give the women whose stories these are a good shake and tell them to buck up. Surely men – however painfully British they might be – aren't allowing their lives to be dictated by a fear of rudeness?

There's no denying that there are a lot of stories in this book from women who should have just told everyone to fuck off, and that can be frustrating to read; but it's also, I'm afraid, a reflection of the reality of being a woman. There's no one with whom I've felt so exasperated in the writing of this book as myself. If you met me, you would probably describe me as confident (which might be a euphemism for loud); I certainly have more self-belief than most women. I know I'm bright, I think I'm fairly successful, and despite what a lot of men on Reddit say, I reckon I'm quite pretty, and yet I've managed to fill a fair bit of the book with stories of times when I was unable to be honest about how I felt or what I needed.

The entire time I was writing, a voice at the back of my head kept saying, 'Why should *we* have to change? Why should *we* have to be the ones who fix a world which is currently designed to fuck us over?' It doesn't seem right that we're indoctrinated into a cult of passivity, and then obliged to fight that nature and improve on it. And, of course, we shouldn't have to. But if we don't, no one else will. Unfortunately, and unfairly, harnessing the power of rude is a lot about accepting that the way things are, and the way things should be, are often not one and the same, and that your options are to complain about the system or to try to change it.

In July 2017, Gina Martin was up-skirted at a Killers concert – a man took a picture up her skirt without her consent. When she reported it to the police, she was told that there was nothing they could do. At the time, if you took a picture up someone's skirt and they were wearing underwear, it wasn't a so-called 'graphic image' and therefore was not illegal. Frustrated by this ridiculous piece of law, Gina decided to turn her anger to action. She posted about it online, wrote articles about it, spoke publicly again and again, and together, with the lawyer Ryan Whelan, she ended up changing the law. Her anger at her experience made the world safer for women and girls, which is the exact kind of radically 'rude' behaviour that we so desperately need. In her book *Be The Change: A Toolkit for the Activist in You*, she writes: 'Without any political or legal experience, I have changed the law. Me! A regular, working-class person with a full-time job. I got very mediocre grades in school and I always said that the only industry I'd refuse to go into was politics. I'm also so spectacularly disorganised that in the last decade I've lost twenty debit cards. If I can change the law, you can to.'

I'm not for a second saying that it is easy. If you read Gina's book you'll see that it took thousands of hours of getting up early, staying up late, missing things she wanted to do and prioritising her activism above other things, but it is possible. If we, as women, stop accepting that things are the way they are, even when they are frustrating or unfair or debilitating, then there is genuinely no limit to what we can change.

*

All the time I was writing *The Power of Rude* I feared people leaving reviews claiming that it portrays women as weak. Not because I'm vain and care what people write about me on Amazon (though that part is absolutely true), but because I think this book demonstrates how long-suffering, brave and emotionally resilient women can be. Despite the fact that we have structured our lives to avoid being victims of violence or abuse, despite the fact that we have to work harder and contort ourselves into positions to fit into the world around us, we still keep on keeping on. I really do consider myself to be a ballsy, strong, intelligent woman. And yet, it's right here in black and white that, time and time again, I've been weak: I've chosen the path of least resistance; I've let people use me, treat me badly, hurt me and kick me around emotionally, because it was easier than the alternative. That doesn't mean that I am a problem. Nor does it mean that any of the other women who so generously donated their stories to this book are weak. None of us are. We're just trying to live in a world that has a very specific set of expectations of our behaviour and punishes those who transgress.

While writing the chapters on sex and dating, I was knocked for six by the sheer number of women who have suffered for having the audacity to reject a man without a buttercream-icing-and-sprinkles excuse. It seems as if the general perception is that women should be strong, ballsy and brave, that we should ask for what we want and stand up for ourselves when we're treated badly; but when we do that, we're punished for it – we're written off as bitches and divas at work and we're physically endangered in our personal lives. So, depressingly, we find ourselves caught between a need to change our behaviour and a mob with pitchforks and torches ready to condemn us if we actually try to do it.

When I was thinking about the rude role models I wanted to include, I really struggled. The modern women who are famously rude are ones I wouldn't regard as inspirational – women like Katie Hopkins and Julia Hartley-Brewer, who deliberately seek to say the things that no one else will in order to get a reaction. Hopkins's autobiography is even called *Rude*. I hate that women see their options as being to smile nicely and pretend to be happy all the time, or to fall into that model of behaviour where upsetting people is a daily aim rather than an undesirable occasional necessity.

I'm far from the first person to conflate feminism and rudeness, nor am I the first to see an essential correlation between the two, but often the sentiment seems to be that women are just being a bit wet. There are plenty of high-profile feminists who enjoy talking about how pathetic modern women have become, how we should learn to kick men in the crotch rather than 'letting' them push us into sex. I agree with them that rudeness is something that women could do well to embrace, but I cannot tolerate the idea that it's somehow our fault if we can't, and that we should be held responsible for a message that was drummed into us from childhood.

The hardest part of writing this book was finding a happy, tied-up-with-a-bow conclusion to the problem that in being rude, you may initially find yourself punished rather than rewarded. Like most people, I like to hope that if you do the 'right' thing, people will approve of it. I want to be liked more than almost anything else in the world. But when it comes to being rude, that just isn't the case. The 'right' thing will almost always be the harder one. The one which winds other people up, gets you criticised or maligned. The rude way is, almost always, the hard way.

If you finish this book and decide to stop saying yes when you mean no, turn down a bridesmaid role that you can't afford or don't want, demand a pay rise or tell your boyfriend that you've been faking your orgasms for the last two years, I cannot pretend that it's going to go down well. The people in your life who have been made happy by you doing what they want, rather than what you want, will not be pleased. It might lead to arguments, break-ups, friendship schisms and work problems. People who used to call you 'sweet' might stop doing so, and you need to ask yourself how you feel about that. Do you want to be 'sweet'? Or do you want to do what you want, when you want?

Being rude doesn't have to be an all-or-nothing choice. When I wrote the Taylor Swift pages, I was struck by what a diametric person she is – both hyper-feminine, sweet and polite and ball-breaking and businesslike. She picks and chooses her moments to embrace the power of rude, and you can do the same thing. You are not obliged to view rudeness as a religion. I would suggest that it's more like a superpower, something that you deploy as and when you need it.

My hope is that one day, probably a long time from now, your daughter, or goddaughter, or niece, will pick up this book and flick through it, and find that she is completely unable to understand any of the stories I've recounted; totally baffled by the idea that any woman would behave in a way that left her feeling sad or ashamed because she didn't think she had permission to do otherwise.

FURTHER READING

Tallulah: My Autobiography by Tallulah Bankhead (University Press of Mississippi, 2004)

Ma'am Darling: 99 Glimpses of Princess Margaret by Craig Brown (Fourth Estate, 2017)

Why Men Earn More: The Startling Truth Behind the Pay Gap – And What Women Can Do About It by Warren Farrell (Amacom, 2005)

The Favourite: Sarah, Duchess of Marlborough by Ophelia Field (Sceptre, 2003)

Rosa Parks: My Story by Jim Haskins and Rosa Parks (Puffin, 1999)

How the Pill Changes Everything: Your Brain on Birth Control by Sarah E. Hill (Orion Spring, 2019)

The Secret Diaries of Miss Anne Lister, vol. 1: I Know My Own Heart by Anne Lister, ed. Helena Whitbread (Virago, 2010)

All That Glitters: Anna Wintour, Tina Brown, and the Rivalry Inside America's Richest Media Empire by Thomas Maier (Skyhorse, 2019)

Be The Change: A Toolkit for the Activist in You by Gina Martin (Sphere, 2019)

The Second Shift: Working Families and the Revolution at Home by Arlie Russell Hochschild (Penguin, 2012)

No One Is Too Small to Make a Difference by Greta Thunberg (Penguin, 2019)

Queen Bees and Wannabes: Helping Your Daughter Survive Cliques, Gossip, Boyfriends and the Realities of Girl World by Rosalind Wiseman (Piatkus, 2004)

ACKNOWLEDGEMENTS

I rather flippantly dedicated *The Power of Rude* to myself, because I think it's fair to say that I did a lot of the heavy lifting on it. I share the dedication with my sister, who is the least rude woman I know. We were sitting outside drinking wine in the snow, in Devon, in February (a long story), and I told her that I wanted to turn my experience of being a brief national news story into a non-fiction book. We'd been kicking around ideas as to what I could write about, and when I described this one her face lit up: 'That's the one,' she told me. 'You need to write that.' So, I did. Thanks Lucy.

Writing a book takes a lot more people than I had ever anticipated. First my amazing agent, Eve White, who has shepherded me through the whole process since I was a twenty-three-year-old student, alongside Ludo Cinelli. Then the entire team at Trapeze, who welcomed me as a new author writing non-fiction for the first time.

I also need to thank the entire early pregnancy unit team at the Elizabeth Garrett Anderson wing of UCL hospital, who looked after me with such compassion during some of the darkest days of my life.

I promised my mortgage advisor, David Hutchinson, that if he managed to get my mortgage approved, I'd mention him here. You're a wizard, David. Thank you for the flat.

I'd also like to thank Layla, Ivy and Erin, respectively three years old, two and a half years old and ten months old at time of writing. When I thought about my hope for this book, it was that you three never make the same choices that I did, or at least that you make them because you want to rather than in obligation.

Then, of course, the always list, the people who kept me sane, listened to me complain bitterly about trying to write a book while having a full-time job: My perfect, brilliant parents Tim and Charlotte, my beloved siblings Lucy and George, and my incomparable friends: Flick, Hannah C., Steph (sorry for taking you out of the acknowledgements for *Perfect Liars*), Ieuan, Aimee, Georgie, Carol, Rebecca and Felix, Ian, Katie, Rob, Natalia, Ed, Juliette, Madeleine, Graham, Natalie, Rob, Liv, Grace, Kathy, Emily, Mel, Chloe, Pete, Emma, Jon, Darcy, Ellen, Miranda, Jess, Lisa, Faima, and all my glorious Sillars cousins.

Lastly, of course, my husband Marcus, who pours the wine, wipes away the tears, takes my ASOS returns to the post office and never gets cross when I invite twelve people to an impromptu dinner. I love you. Thank you for choosing such a rude wife.

ABOUT THE AUTHOR

Rebecca Reid is an author and journalist, and the former digital editor of *Grazia* magazine. She has written for the *Telegraph*, *Stylist*, the *Guardian*, the *Independent* and *Marie Claire*, amongst others. She is a regular on *Good Morning Britain*, *5 News* and *Sky News*, and has previously appeared on *Woman's Hour* and *This Morning*. Her novels include *Perfect Liars* and *Truth Hurts*.

She lives in North London with her husband.

CREDITS

Trapeze would like to thank everyone at Orion who worked on the publication of *The Power of Rude* in the UK.

Editor
Vicky Eribo

Copy-editor
Linden Lawson

Proofreader
Sally Sargeant

Editorial Management
Rosie Pearce
Jane Hughes
Alice Davis
Claire Boyle

Audio
Paul Stark
Amber Bates

Contracts
Paul Bulos
Anne Goddard
Ellie Bowker

Production
Katie Horrocks
Fiona McIntosh

Design
Debbie Holmes
Joanna Ridley
Helen Ewing

Finance
Jennifer Muchan
Jasdip Nandra
Sue Baker

Marketing
Lucy Cameron

Publicity
Francesca Pearce

Sales
Laura Fletcher
Jen Wilson
Victoria Laws
Esther Waters

Frances Doyle
Georgina Cutler
Jack Hallam
Barbara Ronan
Dominic Smith
Deborah Deyong
Lauren Buck
Maggy Park

Operations
Jo Jacobs
Sharon Willis
Lisa Pryde
Lucy Brem

Rights
Susan Howe
Richard King
Krystyna Kujawinska
Jessica Purdue
Louise Henderson

Help us make the next generation of readers

We – both author and publisher – hope you enjoyed this book. We believe that you can become a reader at any time in your life, but we'd love your help to give the next generation a head start.

Did you know that 9 per cent of children don't have a book of their own in their home, rising to 13 per cent in disadvantaged families*? We'd like to try to change that by asking you to consider the role you could play in helping to build readers of the future.

We'd love you to think of sharing, borrowing, reading, buying or talking about a book with a child in your life and spreading the love of reading. We want to make sure the next generation continue to have access to books, wherever they come from.

And if you would like to consider donating to charities that help fund literacy projects, find out more at **www.literacytrust.org.uk** and **www.booktrust.org.uk**.

THANK YOU

*As reported by the National Literacy Trust